THE LAW
(IN PLAIN ENGLISH)®
FOR CRAFTSPEOPLE

LEONARD D. DUBOFF

A COPELAND PRESS BOOK
HARTLEY & MARKS, Publishers

Co-published by

Copeland Press, Inc.
P.O. Box 1992
Wilmington, Delaware 19899

and

Hartley & Marks, Inc., Publishers
Box 147
Point Roberts, Washington 98281

ISBN 0-88179-032-X

If not available at your local bookstore,
this book may be ordered from the publisher.
Send the cover price plus one dollar
fifty for shipping to Hartley & Marks, Inc.

LIBRARY OF CONGRESS CATALOGING-IN-PUBLICATION DATA

DuBoff, Leonard D.
The Law (in plain English) for Craftspeople

Includes index.
1. Law- United States. 2. Artisans - Legal status, laws, etc.-
United States.
3. Artisans - United States - Handbooks, manuals, etc.
I. Title
KF390.A69D8 1991 349.73'024331794 91-7886
347.30024331794

TABLE OF CONTENTS

FOREWORD

Too often, our failure to succeed as craft professionals lies *not* in the absence of talent or skills but in resistance to acquiring a knowledge of sound business practices—especially those related to law and contracts. Like it or not, artists and artisans are as involved as other professionals in business and business law. Because art is at best a precarious means of life support, we require familiarity with law in order to proceed easily and confidently in business transactions.

We have a perennial tendency to spurn all conventional wisdom, to treat business dealings with the same spirit of adventure with which we develop media or style. Reinventing the wheel of business practice does not work as well as we would like, and being unclear in contractual matters makes us the more vulnerable in transactions in which we commit our resources and our future.

We confuse probing experimentally *with* a medium with methods of negotiating *outside* it, that is with *others*. Within media we make, in a brief period, many trials and many errors; we learn from the direct cause-and-effect typical of craft process, and move on. Because business transactions involve additional elements (notably other people, *their* practices, *their* memory and mores), we must learn how to deal directly and successfully with them.

Because I learned too slowly the implications of business law and am only recently as at ease with contracts as with craft, I am pleased about this book. Now all of us can learn from others' experience—interpreted specifically for our special audience. Here it is, a viable tool in itself and invaluable to the Standards of Practice that the American Craft Council is (at last) developing.

Jack Lenor Larsen, *President*
American Craft Council

PREFACE

During the past two decades, the bonding of two apparently dissimilar fields, art and law, has taken place. While it is impossible to identify the precise point when the union of these two professions began, it is easy to spot several evens that were significant in bringing about the merger. For some curious reason the factors that contributed to what is today recognized as the discipline of Artlaw were spontaneous, covering a broad geographic area and in some cases occurring simultaneously.

For example, in 1969 three New York lawyers perceived that creative people needed a special kind of legal representation that was not then available. These attorneys formed the Volunteer Lawyers for the Arts (VLA). The organization was recognized by the New York Bar and within a relatively short period of time VLA enlisted a large number of attorneys.

The organization has three major objectives. First, it acts as a network among those lawyers who are willing to contribute time to aiding artists with art-related legal problems; second, it attempts to educate individuals interested in the field of Artlaw; and third, it serves as a leader in the field of Artlaw by publishing practical guides to new developments in the area.

The Volunteer Lawyers for the Arts concept spread rapidly throughout the United States, and today there is a coast-to-coast network of VLA organizations. While the movement has not yet reached every state, the trend is obvious and every year other organizations join the ranks.

The evolutionary process that resulted in the Artlaw discipline involved educators as well as lawyers. Students in many colleges and universities are now being offered an opportunity to take courses in this field on both undergraduate and graduate levels.

In 1975 the Association of American Law Schools created an

Artlaw section, thus providing law professors with a forum within which to exchange ideas about the field. Today, many law students are being trained as art lawyers.

The increase in activity in this emerging area has even reached legislators. Laws on art, at both federal and state levels, are appearing at an increasing rate.

Periodicals and professional journals such as *The Crafts Report* regularly carry articles on the law as it affects artists and craftspeople, and these articles have been very well received. Although several books on Artlaw are now available to attorneys, very little has been published that is up to date and specifically aimed at the needs and interests of professional craftspeople.

The material in this volume is based to a large extent on articles that have been published previously, primarily in *The Crafts Report*. The information has been updated and integrated so as to provide professional craftmakers with a comprehensive single volume that deals with the field of crafts law as of 1991. The numerous changes in copyright, trademark, tax and corporate law which have occurred in recent years have been included in this volume. In addition, to the laws which have impact on craftspeople, case law interpretation of those laws is also discussed in plain English.

The project of compiling the source material and working on the revisions of this volume was the result of numerous individual efforts. I would like to extend my special thanks to Pat Maloney, J.D.; Shelly Nikodem, J.D. 1990; and my law school colleagues Larry Brown and Jack Bogdanski. I would also like to thank Lammot Copeland, publisher of *The Crafts Report*, and his staff particularly Deborah Copeland, Fred Kessler, Betty Hahn and John Monaghan for their helpful comments and editorial assistance. Lenair Mulford of the Lewis and Clark Law School staff deserves special recognition for weaving my often illegible notes into a neatly typed manuscript.

I am also indebted to the late Michael Scott for encouraging me to write this book. Michael's leadership in the crafts industry as long-time Editor of *The Crafts Report* is well recognized and sorely missed.

Finally, I would like to acknowledge the invaluable assistance of my partner in law and in life, Mary Ann Crawford DuBoff. Without her tireless efforts this project would never have been completed.

Leonard D. DuBoff

INTRODUCTION

How I wish that this book was available when my work as an individual woodworker commenced.

Leonad DuBoff, in this third edition, has answered the problems and questions that confronted me many times as I struggled in my early years.

As designers and makers, we become so immersed in our work, often too idealistic, until a problem confronts us that we do not comprehend and only then does reality become a part of our work.

I found each area in this edition very helpful to me—even after many years of working as I do.

Though I have worked and conducted my workshop by trial and error and though I have been very impulsive in my working and business decisions over the last forty-five years—and it has worked for me—how much easier and more beneficial it would have been for me had I been able to receive instruction from such a book as this.

To this day, I negotiate all of my business contracts myself. Would I change? No! But if I were starting a career in any of the craft or art medias and was concerned about the realities in life in the business world—and it is a business if you are depending on whatever skills you may have to sustain you—then I would try and learn as much as possible about the good and bad aspects of being my own employer.

This book contains so many answers to questions that have confronted me as a professional craftsman that I feel it should be on every artist and craftsman's bookshelf, as it will be on mine.

Sam Maloof*
Woodworker, Fellow
MacArthur Foundation

Sam Maloof is now living in Alta Loma, California. He was the past President of the Southern California Designer and a past Trustee of the Southeast Region of the American Crafts Council. As a world-renowned craftsperson, Sam has received the John D. and Catherine T. MacArthur Foundation Fellowship, as well as numerous other prestigious awards. He is a writer, teacher, jurist and scholar.

To my partner in law and in life, Mary Ann Crawford DuBoff, and to my children, Colleen Rose, Robert Courtney and Sabrina Ashley.

1

FORMS OF
ORGANIZATION

Many craftworkers are particularly happy in their profession because they believe they have escaped the stultifying atmosphere of the grey-suit business world. But they have not escaped it entirely. The same laws that govern the billion-dollar auto industry govern the craftsperson. In this chapter on organizing a small business, I will show ways of using business law to your advantage.

In order to survive in business, all craftworkers know they must carefully plan their money matters, yet few craftmakers realize the importance of planning the *form* of the business enterprise itself. Most craftspeople have little need of the sophisticated organizational structure used in industry. But since craftspeople must pay taxes, take out loans, and expose themselves to uncertain liabilities with every sale they make, it only makes sense to structure the business in such a way as to minimize these worries.

Every business has an organizational form best suited to it. When I counsel craftspeople on organizing their businesses, I usually go about it in two steps. First, we discuss various aspects of tax and liability in order to decide which of the basic forms is best. There are only a handful of basic forms: the *sole proprietorship*, the *partnership*, the *corporation*, and a few hybrids. Once we decide which of these is appropriate, we can go into the organizational details like partnership agreements or corporate bylaws. These define the day-to-day operations of the business and, therefore, must be tailored to individual situations.

What I propose to do here is explain some of the basic features of typical business organizations with respect to their advantages and disadvantages. This should put you in a good position to decide for yourself which form is best for you.

Much of what follows will anticipate problems but, since full discussion of the more intricate details cannot be given here, a craftsmaker should consult an attorney before attempting to adopt any particular structure. My main purpose here is to assist you in communicating your wishes to your lawyer and enable you to understand the choices available.

THE AMERICAN DREAM: SOLE PROPRIETORSHIP

The technical name for this form of business may be unfamiliar to you, but chances are it is the form under which you operate now. The sole proprietorship is an unincorporated business owned by one person. Though not peculiar to the United States, it was, and still is, the essence of the American dream—for personal freedom follows economic freedom. As a form of business it is elegant in its simplicity. All that it requires is a little money and a little work. Legal requirements are few and simple. In most localities, in order to operate a business, you must obtain a license from the city or county, which usually entails no more than paying a small fee. If you wish to operate the business under a name other than your own, the name must be registered with the state, and in some cases, the county in which you are doing business. With these details taken care of, you are in business.

DISADVANTAGES OF SOLE PROPRIETORSHIP

There are numerous pitfalls involved in operating your business as a sole proprietor. If these dangers are sufficiently real in your case, you probably should consider some of the alternative forms of organization discussed later in this chapter.

If you are the sole proprietor of a venture, your personal property is at stake. If for any reason you owe more than the dollar value of your business, your creditors can take most of your personal property to satisfy the debt. In many cases, insurance can be obtained that will shift the loss from you to the insurance company. But there are some risks for which no insurance can be obtained. For instance, no insurance can be purchased to protect against a large rise in cost or sudden unavailability of materials. Insurance premiums can be quite high, and it is impossible to predict premium increases. These as well as many other factors can drive a small business, and thus the sole proprietor, into bankruptcy.

TAXES

Before leaving the area of the sole proprietor, I must briefly deal with taxes. The sole proprietor is taxed on all business profits and may deduct losses. The rate of tax paid will increase as income increases. Fortunately, there are some methods to lessen this tax burden. For instance, you can establish an approved pension plan, deduct a specified amount of your net income, and put that money in an interest-bearing account or in approved government securities or mutual funds. You can withdraw these funds when you are in a lower tax bracket; however, there are several restrictions and penalties if you withdraw this money prior to retirement age.

PARTNERSHIP

A partnership is defined by most state laws as an association of two or more persons to conduct, as co-owners, a business for profit. It can be an attractive arrangement because partners pool money, supplies and professional contacts. No formalities are required by the definition. In fact, there are cases where people have been held to be partners even though they had no intention of forming a partnership. For example, if you lend a friend some money to start a business and the friend agrees to pay you a certain percentage of whatever profit is made, you may be your friend's partner in the eyes of the law even though you take no further interest in the business. This is important because each partner is subject to unlimited personal liability for the debts of the partnership. Also, each partner is liable for the negligence of another partner and of the partnership's employees when the negligent act occurred in the usual course of business. In effect, each partner is considered an employee of the partnership.

From this, two things should be obvious. First, since the addition of a partner increases your potential liability, some care should be exercised in finding a responsible partner. Second, the partnership should be adequately insured to protect both the assets of the partnership and the personal assets of each partner. It is a good idea to draw up a written partnership agreement to avoid future confusion or misunderstandings.

As mentioned above, no formalities are required to create a partnership. Where there is no formal agreement defining the terms of the partnership, such as control of the partnership or the distribution of profits, state law supplies the terms. The state laws are based on the fundamental characteristics of the typical partnership throughout the ages and are, therefore, thought to correspond to the reasonable expectations of the partners. The most important of these presumed characteristics are:

1. No one can become a member of a partnership without the unanimous consent of all partners;
2. All members have an equal vote in the management of the partnership regardless of the size of their interest in it;
3. All partners share equally in the profits and losses of the partnership no matter how much capital they contribute;
4. A simple majority vote is required for decisions in the ordi-

nary course of business, and a unanimous vote is required to change the fundamental character of the business; and

5. A partnership is terminable at will by any partner; if a partner withdraws, the partnership is legally dissolved.

Most of these laws contain a provision that allows the partners to make their own agreement in order to work out the management structure and division of profits which best suits the needs of the individual partnership.

MAJOR ITEMS OF AGREEMENT

Some of the major details to be considered in preparing a partnership agreement include: the name of the partnership; a description of the business; contributions of capital by the partners; duration of the partnership; distribution of profits; management responsibilities; duties of partners; prohibited acts; and provisions for the dissolution of the partnership.

As you can see, a comprehensive partnership agreement is no simple matter. It is, in fact, essential for potential partners to devote some time to preparation of an agreement and to enlist the services of a business lawyer. For the initial expense of a lawyer who puts together an agreement suited to the needs of your partnership, you will save many times the legal fees in the smooth organization, operation, and final dissolution of your partnership.

The economic advantages of doing business in a partnership are the pooling of capital, greater ease in obtaining credit because of the collective credit rating, and a potentially more efficient allocation of labor and resources. A major disadvantage is that each partner is fully and personally liable for all the debts of the partnership—even if he or she was not personally involved in incurring those debts.

A partnership does not possess any special tax advantages over a sole proprietorship. As a partner, you will pay a personal income tax on your share of the profits whether they are distributed or not. In turn, each partner is entitled to the same proportion of the partnership deductions and credits. The partnership must prepare for availability to the IRS an annual information return known as Schedule K-1, Form 1065, which details each partner's share of income, credits, and deductions, and against which the IRS can check the individual returns filed by the partners.

THE LIMITED PARTNERSHIP

The limited partnership is a hybrid structure containing elements of both the partnership and corporation. A limited partnership may be formed by parties who wish to invest in a partnership and, in return, to share in its profits, but who seek to limit their risk to the amount of their investment. The law provides for such limited risk, but only so long as the limited partner plays no active role in the day-to-day management and operation of the business. In effect, the limited partner is very much like an investor who buys a few shares of stock in a corporation but has no significant role in running the corporation. Therefore, in order to establish a limited partnership it is necessary to have one or more general partners who run the business and who have full personal liability, and one or more limited partners who must play a passive role.

In order to form a limited partnership, a certificate must be filed with the proper state office. If the certificate is not filed or is improperly filed, the limited partner could be treated as a general partner and thus lose the protection of limited liability. In addition, the limited partner *must* refrain from trying to influence the day-to-day operation of the partnership. Otherwise, the limited partner might be found to be actively participating in the business and thereby held to be a general partner with unlimited liability.

A limited partnership can be used to attract investment when credit is hard to obtain or is too expensive. In return for investing, the limited partner receives a designated share of the profits. If there are no profits, the limited partner receives nothing, whereas a creditor of the partnership can sue if the partners fail to repay.

Another use of the limited partnership is to facilitate reorganization of a general partnership after the death or retirement of a general partner. Rather than liquidating the partnership assets to return the capital contribution, the retired partner (or his heir) can receive the fruits of his past labors but free his personal assets from the risk of loss in a large suit against the partnership.

THE EIGHT BASICS OF A PARTNERSHIP AGREEMENT

THE NAME OF THE PARTNERSHIP
Most partnerships simply use the surnames of the major partners. The choice here is nothing more than the order of names. Various factors can be considered, from prestige to euphony. If a name other than the partners' is used, then it will be necessary to file the assumed business name with the state and possibly with the county. Care should be taken to choose a name which is distinctive and not already in use. If the name is not distinctive, others can copy it; if the name is already in use, you may become liable for trade-name infringement.

A DESCRIPTION OF THE BUSINESS
Here the partners should agree on the basic scope of the business, its requirements of capital and labor, their corresponding contributions of capital and labor, and perhaps some features of any future growth.

PARTNERSHIP CAPITAL
After determining how much capital to contribute, the partners must decide when it is to be contributed, how to value the property contributed, whether there is to be a right to contribute more or to withdraw any at a later date.

DURATION OF THE PARTNERSHIP

Sometimes partnerships are organized for a fixed duration or are automatically dissolved on certain conditions.

DISTRIBUTION OF PROFITS

Any scheme for distribution of profits can be arranged. Although ordinarily a partner does not receive a salary, it is possible to give an active partner a guaranteed salary in addition to a share of the profits. Since the partnership's profits can only be determined at the close of a business year, ordinarily no distribution is made until that time. However, it is possible to allow the partners a monthly draw of money against their final share of profits. In some cases, it may be necessary to allow limited expense accounts for some partners.

Not all of the profits of the partnership need be distributed at year's end. Some can be retained for expansion. This can be provided for in the partnership agreement. It should be noted that whether the profits are distributed or not, each partner must pay tax on his or her designated share. The tax code refers directly to the partnership agreement to determine what constitutes each partner's share, which shows how important a partnership agreement on this is.

MANAGEMENT

The division of power in the partnership can be made in many ways. All partners can be given an equal voice, or some more than others. A few partners may be allowed to manage the business entirely, the remaining partners being given a vote only on pre-designated areas of concern. Besides voting, three other areas of management should be covered. First is the question of who can sign checks, place orders, or sell partnership property. Under state partnership laws, any partner may do these things as long as they are done in the usual course of business. But such a broad delegation of authority can lead to confusion, so it may be best to delegate this authority more narrowly.

Second, it is a good idea to determine a regular date for partnership meetings. Third, some consideration should be given to the unfortunate possibility of a dispute among the partners leading to a deadlock vote. One way to avoid this is to distribute the voting power in such a way as to make a deadlock impossible. But that would mean that in a two-person partnership one partner would be in absolute control, which might be unacceptable to the other partner. If, instead, the power is divided evenly among an even number of partners, as is often the case, the agreement should stipulate a neutral party or arbitrator who can settle the dispute and thereby often avoid a dissolution of the partnership.

PROHIBITED ACTS

Before going into the details of what sort of acts should be prohibited, I must first discuss the three fundamental duties that each partner owes the partnership by virtue of being an employee or agent of the partnership. First is the duty of diligence. This means the partner must exercise reasonable care in acting as a partner. Second is the duty of obedience. The partner must obey the rules that the partnership has promulgated and, more importantly, must not exceed the authority that the partnership has vested in her or him. Finally, there is a duty of loyalty. A partner may not, without approval of the other partners, compete with the partnership in another business. He or she may not seize upon a business opportunity which would be of value to the partnership without first disclosing the opportunity to the partnership and allowing the partnership to pursue it.

A list of acts prohibited to a partner can be drawn up in order to elaborate and expand on these fundamental duties.

DISSOLUTION AND LIQUIDATION

A partnership is automatically dissolved upon the death, withdrawal or expulsion of a partner. Dissolution identifies the legal end of the partnership but need not affect its economic life if the partners provide for the continuation of the business after a dissolution. Nonetheless, a dissolution will affect the business because the partner who withdraws or is expelled, or the estate of a deceased partner, will be entitled to a return of that partner's share of the total capital of the partnership. How this capital is to be returned should be decided before the occurrence, for it may be impossible to negotiate at the time of dissolution.

One method of handling this is to provide for a return of capital in cash over a period of time. After a partner leaves, the partnership may need to be reorganized and recapitalized. Some provision should be made to define in what proportion the remaining partners may purchase the interest of the departed partner. Finally, since it is always possible that the partners will desire to liquidate the partnership, it should be decided in advance who will liquidate the assets, what assets will be distributed as such, and what property will be returned to its original contributor.

WHAT YOU DON'T WANT: UNINTENDED PARTNERS

Whether yours is a straightforward partnership or a limited partnership, one arrangement you want to avoid is the unintended partnership. Following are some examples of the fact that law and art can overlap in the area of horror stories—and why an ounce of prevention, in the form of a moderate legal fee, can sometimes save pounds of money and headaches later.

In 1978, Irene Stein, a well-known Colorado artist, went to Moses Sanchez, a retired welder turned metal sculptor, and showed him a sketch she allegedly had made. The sketch, which bore a remarkable resemblance to Rosak's *Cradle Song, Variation No. Two* [catalogued in the collection of the Museum of Modern Art], was used by Sanchez only for inspiration. The sculpture he ultimately created bore very little resemblance to the original sketch.

Sanchez was outraged some time later when he was shown a newspaper article with a picture of Mrs. Stein wearing a welder's mask, holding a torch and standing in front of his creation, which the article ascribed to her.

Sanchez sued, alleging that he was the artist. Stein defended on the ground that she was the creator and Sanchez was merely a foundryman who embodied her ideas in a tangible metal form. The contrived shot of Mrs. Stein in the newspaper was never fully explained, though Stein suggested that it was the newspaper photographer's idea rather than her own.

The issue presented by this case is by no means a novel one. When, for example, a person commissions a portrait and periodically reviews the artist's progress, recommending additions or changes, can the patron be considered the artist, or at least a collaborator? On the other hand, when the sculptor creates a master image or maquette that is made into a mold and cast by a metal foundry, has the foundryman become co-creator of the work? Similar examples abound in the crafts field—between the stained-glass designer and the craftsman who executes the design, for instance, or the weaver of a commissioned wall hanging, and the interior decorator who specifies its size, theme, color scheme and design.

In an early French case, *Guino c. Consorts, Renoir*, an apprentice in Renoir's studio, Guino, claimed co-authorship of sculptures he had executed under Renoir's direction. The French court concluded that Guino's own personality was sufficiently imprinted on the work so that it could no longer be considered solely Renoir's creation. Unfortunately, the court did not state how much personality Guino had to imprint to entitle him to claim the right of co-authorship.

Towards the end of her life, *Newsweek* magazine reported that Georgia O'Keefe's sight was failing and that she merely signed canvases which had been painted by another. A New Mexico handyman, John Poling, claimed he had painted three O'Keefe canvases under her instruction. O'Keefe admitted that Poling physically made the work, but she claimed that he was merely the equivalent of her palette knife.

Another interesting situation arose several years ago when it was admitted that many portraits, including those of John F. Kennedy, Justice Brandeis and other notables, signed by Charles J. Fox, were actually painted by Irving Resnikoff. Fox admitted paying Resnikoff $250 to $300 for each portrait, which he then sold for up to $7,000 apiece. These admissions were made in tax court where Fox claimed that his profits from the resales were capital gains rather than ordinary income, as the earnings of an artist creating and selling a painting would normally be classified. Fox claimed he did not execute the pieces and therefore should be taxed at the lower capital gains rate. Fox also attempted to take a business deduction for the amount paid Resnikoff, the original artist.

Since Fox probably met with the patron, or obtained a photograph, conceptualized the project and merely had Resnikoff execute the final product, should Fox be considered the artist or at least a co-author? The dilemma presented by the fact that the person who actually executes the work is different from the one who has the original idea is a difficult one.

In *Sanchez v. Stein*, the issue was resolved by the parties themselves prior to the trial. Mrs. Stein admitted that she was not the creator of the now famous metal sculpture of a crescent within which three nested eagles reach skyward, which Moses Sanchez, the actual creator, entitled "Winged Wolves." Stein agreed to pay Sanchez a cash settlement and return several other of his works she had in her possession. It would appear that, in this case at least, the person who created the work was acknowledged as the artist.

In *Community for Creative Non-Violence (CCNV) v. Reid*, the Supreme Court held that the individual who executes the work is considered the artist for copyright purposes, though parties may have agreed before the work began that their individual contributions should result in a joint work (discussed more fully in Chapter 7). Thus the surest way to avoid unintended partners is to spell out, in a detailed writing, the essentials and expectations of any business arrangement you enter into with another person.

THE CORPORATION

The corporation may sound like a form of business that pertains only to large manufacturers with many employees—an impersonal monster wholly alien to the world of the craftsperson. Whether or not this image corresponds to reality, in essence there is nothing in the nature of the corporation that requires it. There are advantages and disadvantages to incorporating. If it appears advantageous to incorporate, it can be done with surprising ease and with little expense. Nonetheless, it is necessary to use a lawyer's assistance to ensure that the formalities required by the state are fulfilled and to be instructed on how to use the corporate machinery and to pay the corporation's taxes.

DIFFERENCES BETWEEN A CORPORATION AND A PARTNERSHIP

In order to discuss the corporation, it is useful to contrast its characteristics with those of a partnership. Perhaps the most important difference is that, like a limited partner, the owners of the corporation, or shareholders as they are commonly called, are not personally liable for the corporation's debts; they stand to lose only their investment. But unlike a limited partner, a shareholder is allowed full participation in the control of the corporation through the shareholders' voting privileges. This limited liability may be partially illusory for the small corporation, however, because very often creditors will demand that the owners personally co-sign for any credit extended.

Individuals are personally liable for their wrongful acts, even if incorporated. An individual is protected by the corporate liability shield if the other contracting party has agreed to hold only the corporation responsible. The corporate liability shield also extends to the wrongful acts of corporate employees. For example, if an assistant negligently injures another person while driving to the clay supplier, the assistant will be liable for the negligent act, and the corporation may be liable as well. The craftsperson who owns the corporation, however, will probably not be personally liable.

The second area of difference is in continuity of existence. The many events which can cause the dissolution of a partnership do not have the same result when they occur within the corporate context. It is common to create a corporation with perpetual existence. Unlike partners, shareholders cannot decide to withdraw and demand a return of their capital from the corporation; their recourse is to sell their stock, which has no direct impact on the capital of the corporation itself. Therefore, a corporation may have legal as well as economic continuity. But, this can also be a tremendous disadvantage to shareholders or their heirs when a sale of stock is desired and there is no one who wishes to buy the stock. However, there are agreements which may be used to guarantee a return of capital should the shareholder die or wish to withdraw.

The third difference is the free transferability of ownership. In a partnership, no one can become a partner without unanimous consent of the other partner(s), unless otherwise agreed. In a corporation, however, shareholders can generally sell their shares to whomever they wish. If a small corporation does not want to be open to outside ownership, this unlimited transferability may be restricted.

The fourth difference is in the structure of management and control. Common shareholders are given a vote in proportion to their ownership in the corporation. There are other kinds of stock that can be created that may or may not have voting rights. A voting shareholder uses his or her vote to elect a board of directors and to create rules under which the board may operate.

The basic rules of the corporation are put in the articles of incorporation which are filed with the state. These serve as a sort of constitution and can be amended by shareholder vote. More detailed operational rules, called bylaws, should also be prepared. Both shareholders and directors may have power to create or amend bylaws. This varies from state to state and may be determined by the shareholders themselves. The board of directors then makes operational decisions of the corporation and may delegate day-to-day control to a president.

A shareholder, even if he or she owns all the stock, may not directly preempt the decision of the board of directors. If the board has exceeded the powers granted to it by the articles or bylaws, any shareholder may use the courts to prevent the action. If the board is within its powers, the shareholders have no recourse except to remove the board or any board member. In a few more progressive states, a small corporation may entirely forego having a board of directors. In such cases, the corporation is authorized to allow the shareholders to vote on business decisions just as in a partnership.

The fifth distinction between a partnership and a corporation is the greater variety of means available to raise additional capital. Partnerships are quite restricted in this regard; they can borrow money or, if all partners agree, they can take on additional partners. A corporation, on the other hand, may issue more stock and this stock can be of many different varieties: recallable at a set price, for example, or convertible into another kind of stock.

A means frequently used to attract a new investor is to issue preferred stock. By this, the corporation agrees to pay the preferred shareholder a predetermined amount before it pays any dividends to other shareholders. Also, if the corporation should go bankrupt, a preferred shareholder will be paid out of the proceeds of liquidation before common shareholders, although after the corporation's general creditors are paid.

The issuance of new stock merely requires, in most cases, approval by a majority of the existing shareholders. In addition, corporations can borrow money on a short-term basis by issuing notes, or for a longer period by issuing debentures or bonds. In fact, a corporation's ability to raise additional capital is only limited by its lawyer's creativity and the economic reality of the marketplace.

The last distinction is the manner in which a corporation is taxed. Under both state and federal laws, the profits of the corporation are taxed before they are paid out as dividends. The dividends constitute personal income to the shareholders and are taxed again as such. This double taxation constitutes the major disadvantage of incorporating.

AVOIDING DOUBLE TAXATION

There are several methods of avoiding double taxation. First, a corporation can plan its business so as not to show very much profit. This can be done by drawing off what would be profit in payments to shareholders in other capacities. For example, a shareholder can be paid a salary for his or her services, rent for property leased to the corporation, or interest on a loan made to the corporation. All of these are legal deductions from the corporate income.

The corporation can also obtain larger deductions for the various health and retirement benefits provided for its employees than can an individual or a partnership. For example, a corporation can deduct all of its payments made for an employee health plan while at the same time the employee does not pay any personal income tax on this. Whereas, sole proprietors or partnerships can deduct only a portion of these expenses.

The corporation can also reinvest its profits for reasonable business expansion. This undistributed money is not taxed as income to the individual as it would be if earned by a partnership, which does not distribute it.

This reinvestment has two advantages. First, the business can be built up with money which has been taxed only at the corporate rate for the first $50,000 of corporate earnings, although the corporate rate is higher for earnings in excess of $50,000. Second, the owner can delay the liquidation and distribution of corporate assets until a time of lower personal income and therefore lower tax rates. There is a possible third advantage, but it comes and goes with the political winds. Money received when a corporation is later liquidated or sold may be characterized as *capital gains*. Congress has, at times, lowered the capital gains tax rate, making this characterization advantageous.

Congress has created a hybrid organizational form which allows the owners of a small corporation to take advantage of many of the features described above in order to avoid the double taxation problem. This form of organization is called an *S Corporation*. If the corporation meets certain requirements, which many small businesses do, the owners can elect to be taxed as a partnership. This can be particularly advantageous in the early years of a corporation because the owners of an S Corporation can deduct the losses of the corporation from their personal income, which is not permissible in a regular corporation (C Corporation). They can achieve this favorable tax situation while enjoying the corporation's limited liability status.

PRECAUTIONS FOR MINORITY SHAREHOLDERS

Dissolving a corporation is not only painful because of certain tax penalties, but it is almost always impossible without the consent of the majority of the shareholders. If you are forming a corporation and will be a minority shareholder, you must realize that the majority will have ultimate and absolute control unless minority shareholders take certain precautions from the start. There are numerous horror stories of what the majority shareholders have done to the minority shareholders. Avoiding these problems is no more difficult than drafting a sort of partnership agreement among the shareholders. I recommend that you retain your own attorney to represent you during the corporation's formation rather than waiting until it is too late.

Additional discussion of corporate tax situations can be found in the chapter on taxes.

2

TRADEMARKS

Although modern trademark law is a relatively new development, its historical antecedents date back to medieval England. In those days certain craft guilds often required their members to place their individual marks on the products they produced so that, in the event a product proved defective, the guild could trace its origins to a particular craftsperson and impose appropriate sanctions. As such, the use of marks enabled the guild to maintain the integrity of its name. Moreover, merchants would often affix marks to their products for purposes of identification. If the product was stolen or misplaced, the merchant could prove ownership by reason of the mark.

The use of marks for purposes of identification would no doubt have worked quite well in an ideal society where all the citizens led principled and moral lives. But such was not the case. Thus, it is not particularly surprising that unscrupulous merchants quickly realized that there was easy money to be made from the use of another's mark, or one confusingly similar. The shoddy craftmakers could more readily sell their products by affixing to them the marks belonging to quality craftworkers.

It was in response to this problem of consumer deception that the first trademark laws were developed in the United States.

Initially the emphasis was on prevention of one person passing off his or her product as that of another. In contrast, modern American law, both common and statutory, focuses upon whether one mark is sufficiently similar to another to cause confusion in the minds of the buying public. The emphasis has thus shifted from the subjective intent of a dishonest craftmaker passing off goods as those of another to the objective determination of consumer confusion.

Despite these changes, the essential purposes of trademarks and trademark laws have changed little since the days of the craft guilds. As discussed below, trademarks still function primarily as a means of identifying the source of a particular product. Moreover, trademark laws are designed to enable the trademark proprietor to develop goodwill for the product as well as to prevent another party from exploiting that goodwill—regardless of whether that exploitation is intentional or innocent.

NEED FOR A RECOGNIZABLE MARK

What, then, is a trademark? A trademark is defined as any word, name, symbol, device or any combination thereof, used by a merchant or manufacturer of a product to identify his or her goods and to distinguish them from the products of competitors. A trademark benefits the public by indicating the source of the product and helps guide wise purchasing. Manufacturers benefit by using the trademark as a marketing and advertising tool. The key to obtaining protection for a trademark lies in the notion that the trademark must be distinguishable.

The level of protection for a trademark varies with the distinctiveness of the mark. The most distinctive marks are *fanciful* or *arbitrary*. A fanciful mark is one that has no meaning in the language apart from its use as a trademark. The mark *Kodak* to identify photographic supplies and equipment for example is fanciful.

Arbitrary marks differ from fanciful marks in that the words are found in the dictionary; however, just as with fanciful marks, there is no relationship between the mark and the product it identifies. *Shell*, the trademark of the petroleum company, is an arbitrary mark because, although it is a dictionary-defined word, its meaning bears no resemblance to the products it identifies. Fanciful and arbitrary marks are accorded substantial protection by trademark laws.

Suggestive marks—marks that are somewhat descriptive of the product but also require some imagination in order to make the connection—are also protected by trademark laws. *Skin-visible* is suggestive of a transparent, adhesive medical tape and thus is a valid and protectable mark. The level of protection may be less, however, if it is easier to claim that the mark is really descriptive because descriptive marks are not afforded legal protection. These marks merely describe the general attributes or qualities of a product. *Raisin Bran*, for example, is the mark for the cereal made of bran flakes and raisins.

Descriptive marks can be protected only if the trademark proprietor can prove that the mark has acquired a secondary meaning. A secondary meaning exists when the public no longer connects the trademark words with their dictionary meaning, but rather connects the mark with the product it identifies. For example, *TV Guide* has probably acquired a secondary meaning as the mark of a specific publication which lists television programs and publishes topical articles about the television industry.

Trademarks that merely identify the product for what it is are *generic* marks. The trademark *Beer* to identify beer is a generic mark and, as such, is not protected by trademark law.

In the *Leathersmiths of London* case, however, the question was whether the name Leathersmiths of London was a protected trademark. The court held that the word *leathersmith* is generic, at least when used to describe someone who is in the business of working with leather, and is therefore not entitled to trademark protection.

Trademarks that become generic through usage, such as *aspirin*, lose their protection. However, if the mark becomes generic with respect to some, but not all goods, the proprietor can petition to have registration cancelled only as to those goods. Manufacturers can lessen the likelihood of this possibility by using arbitrary or fanciful terms in conjunction with any generic or descriptive term they intend to use. It is also a good idea to be cautious in advertising and promotional activities.

Some trademarks, even though considered distinctive, are nevertheless prohibited by statute or public policy. Thus, obscene or scandalous trademarks are generally denied trademark protection. Similarly, trademarks that are deemed deceptively misdescriptive, such as the mark *Idaho potatoes* to identify potatoes produced somewhere other than Idaho, are also denied protection.

PROTECTING A TRADEMARK

In order to secure common law trademark protection, it is not sufficient to merely adopt a distinctive trademark. The trademark must be *used*. A trademark is deemed to be used when it has been placed in any manner on the products or their containers or the displays associated with them or on any of the tags or labels affixed to the products. Thus, it is not always necessary that the trademark actually be physically affixed to the goods. As long as the trademark is associated with the product at the point of sale in such a way that the product can be readily identified as being derived from a particular source, the trademark may be protected.

Merely listing a trademark in a catalogue, ordering labels bearing the trademark, using the trademark on invoices, or exhibiting trademarked goods at a trade show may not be sufficient, in and of themselves, to constitute use. Use of a trademark *must* be associated with the point of sale.

To ensure common law trademark protection, the trademark proprietor would be well-advised to physically affix the trademark to the product. In this way the product is certain to bear the trademark when and if it is sold.

TRADEMARK LOSS AND INFRINGEMENT

As previously discussed, use is a prerequisite to common law trademark protection. But, some forms of use may result in the loss of a trademark. A number of well-known trademarks such as *Aspirin*, *Thermos* and *Escalator* have been lost as a result of improper usage. Generally, trademark protection is lost as a result of the fact that the mark is used in some capacity other than as an adjective modifying a noun. When a trademark is used as a noun or a verb, it no longer functions to identify the source of the product, but rather becomes the name of the product itself. At that point, the mark becomes generic and is not subject to protection.

Once the trademark has been used and adopted, it falls within the purview of common-law trademark protection. Common law protects the trademark proprietor against someone else subsequently using a trademark that is confusingly similar to that of the proprietor.

This raises the question of when trademarks are considered to be confusingly similar. Generally, trademarks will be confusing if they are similar in sound, appearance, or connotation, particularly if the trademarks are affixed to similar products or if products are marketed throughout the same or similar geographic areas. If, on the other hand, two products bearing similar trademarks are not related or are marketed in different geographic areas, there may not be any infringement.

Thus, a craft shop that distributes its products solely in the Northwest could probably adopt and use a trademark solely in use in the state of Maine, although if the trademark is registered, it is protected nationwide. Moreover, the Northwest craft shop could probably adopt and use a trademark used by a Northwest chainsaw manufacturer. In these situations there may be no infringement since it is not likely that the use of the mark by the Northwest craft shop will confuse the consuming public, since the products are so dissimilar.

It is not necessary to prove actual confusion, i.e., you do not need consumers who will testify that, yes indeed, they were confused by the similar marks. The key is the "likelihood of confusion." Courts will consider the strength of the mark, the similarity of the marks, the goods involved and the market channels, whether the goods are usually bought on impulse or if consideration goes into the decision to buy as well as the intent of the alleged infringer.

When a trademark has been infringed, the trademark proprietor may sue the infringing party for monetary damages and/or for an injunction prohibiting the infringing use. Monetary damages are measured by either the plaintiff's losses or the defendant's profits from the use of the infringing mark. The plaintiff must prove that the infringement resulted in actual confusion or deception of consumers in order to show lost profits. If the infringement is found to be willful and deliberate, punitive damages can be awarded, as well as attorney fees.

When actual damages or profits cannot be shown, or are inconclusive, courts can grant an injunction. Preliminary, pretrial injunctions are rare. The plaintiff must show that (1) he or she is likely to be successful in a court case; (2) there will be irreparable injury if no injunction is issued; (3) this injury outweighs any damage that the defendant might suffer; and (4) the public interest will not be harmed by granting an injunction. Monetary damages may be measured either by the plaintiff's losses resulting from the infringement or by the defendant's profits on the goods bearing the infringing mark.

REGISTERING A TRADEMARK

Thus far, the discussion has revolved around the trademark protection afforded by common law. It should be noted, however, that the trademark proprietor may procure greater protection under federal and state statutes.

The federal statute governing trademarks is known as the Lanham Act. It is not the function of the Lanham Act to grant trademark rights (since those are secured by the common-law, discussed above), but rather to provide a central clearinghouse for existing trademarks via registrations.

The Lanham Act was revised in 1988. Prior to this revision the law required that a trademark be adopted and actually used in commerce before the would-be proprietor could apply for registration. The mark had to be affixed to a product that was sold, shipped or otherwise used in interstate commerce. This system for registration was criticized because it required a large investment of time and money in order to create the mark and the product line, as well as getting the line into the stream of commerce.

The 1988 revision eliminates the "actual use" requirement before one can apply for registration of a mark. To apply for registration, you need only state a "bona fide" intent to use the mark in commerce or in connection with goods in commerce. The Patent and Trademark Office (PTO) reviews the application, looking for similar marks that are at the application stage or are already registered. Once it determines that everything is in order, the PTO will publish the mark in the Official Gazette, and anyone who wishes to object has thirty days in which to do so. (The mark may not be registered until it is actually used, though all of the steps leading to registration, including publication for purposes of giving notice of the new intended use, may be completed.)

If no one objects, or the objections are without merit, the PTO will "allow" the mark and send a notice of allowance. The mark is *not* registered at this point. The applicant has six months after receipt of the notice of allowance to provide the PTO with an affidavit stating that the mark is in commercial use. The PTO must also be provided with a drawing of the mark that complies with the specifications of the Trademark Commissioner, three facsimiles or specimens of the trademark as it is being used in connection with or affixed on goods in commerce, and the filing fee of $175.

If an applicant fails to commence using the mark in commerce within the allowable six-month period, it is possible to obtain an extension for another six months. This extension is au-

tomatic upon application and payment of fee, if submitted before the original six-month period expires. Four additional six-
month extensions are also possible but require, in addition to
application and fee submitted before expiration of the current
six-month period, approval by the PTO upon a showing of good
cause why such extension should be granted. In no event, shall
the period between the date of allowance and the commence-
ment of use of the mark in commerce be permitted to exceed
thirty-six months. In making a request for extension, the applicant must include the following: a verified statement of continued 'bona fide" intent to use the mark in commerce, specifica-
tion as to which classification(s) of goods and services the intent
continues to apply, and inclusion of the required fee, which is
currently $100 per extension, per classification of goods or ser-
vices. Application forms may be obtained by calling the PTO at
703-557-3158.

The initial filing of the application is considered to be constructive use of the mark. This means that your priority for
claiming the mark is measured from the date of application. If
another person applies to register the same or a confusingly similar mark after your application is received, he or she will be denied registration. This is true even if the subsequent applicant
puts the mark into commercial use prior to your doing so, but after your filing date. In effect, this filing allows you to reserve a
mark while you investigate the mark and develop the product.

This "bona fide" intent-to-use registration is a supplement to
the "actual use" system, and not a replacement for it. Appli-
cants may continue to register their marks based on use and, in
fact, no mark is registered until it has been used in commerce.
If you have already used the mark, you must provide the PTO
with a drawing, specimens and the filing fee, along with your
application. The review process occurs and, if no problems are
found, the mark is published in the Official Gazette along with
marks originally filed under the intent-to-use provisions. Marks
published in the gazette which are not opposed within 30 days of
publication will be granted a certificate of registration. Regis-

tration entitles you, as trademark proprietor, to certain benefits in addition to those afforded by common law.

BENEFITS OF REGISTERING

First, the registration enables the proprietor to use the symbol "®" in conjunction with the trademark, which may well deter others from using the mark. Second, registration is established evidence of the registrant's right to the exclusive use of the trademark. Finally, a registered trademark that has been in continuous use for a period of five consecutive years generally becomes incontestable.

Thus, by registering the trademark, the proprietor may secure rights superior to those of a prior but unregistered user, but only if the original user does not object to the registrant's use within five years of registration and the registrant applies for incontestability.

A trademark registration remains in effect for a period of ten years, and may be renewed in additional ten-year increments by filing an application for renewal at least six months prior to the expiration of the preceding ten-year term. This is a change from the twenty-year period of prior law. During the ten-year period, however, proof of continued commercial use must be provided. This proof must be in affidavit form and filed during the sixth year of registration. This allows the Register to be purged of marks not being used.

State trademark statutes generally grant rights similar to those of the Lanham Act, and some grant even greater protection, except that those rights do not extend beyond the borders of the state.

In order to obtain trademark protection under state law, the trademark proprietor must file with the appropriate state officer a trademark application along with documentation similar to that required for federal registration by the Lanham Act. The number of examples of the mark to be furnished may vary from state to state, and the registration fee may also be different.

Obviously, registration can be quite beneficial to a craftmaker who has invested time, money and energy in developing a reputation for quality work. Procuring trademark protection on either the state or federal level may require a considerable amount of time and skill. In this regard an attorney may prove invaluable. An attorney can first determine whether the benefits to be derived from registration justify the expenses. The total costs for trademark registration usually run between $800 to $1,000, not counting artist's fees (if any) to have drawings made. Second, an attorney can research a trademark index to determine if there are any conflicting marks. And finally, an attorney can complete the application and deal with any problems that may occur while it is being processed for registration.

Craftworkers interested in contacting attorneys who specialize in trademark work can consult the Yellow Pages of the telephone directory (look for Patent Attorneys or Patent and Trademark) or consult their state bar associations for some recommendations. The Volunteer Lawyers for the Arts organizations in various states may also be able to assist with referrals.

3

CONTRACTS

Craftspeople today are becoming more and more aware of the legal and practical problems that affect them as entrepreneurs. In this chapter we will focus on one of the most fundamental of these—contract law. Clearly, we cannot cover the entire field of contract law, but perhaps I can help readers become aware of some of the law's ramifications and enable you to see where you need protection. Specifically, then, I hope to make you aware of the legal consequences which may flow from the varied transactions among craftspeople, dealers, galleries, employees, tax collectors, public agencies, and consumers or collectors.

WHAT IS A CONTRACT?

A contract is defined as a legally binding promise or set of promises. The law requires the participants in a contract to perform the promises they have made to each other. In the event of nonperformance—usually called a *breach*—the law provides remedies to the injured party. For the purposes of this discussion, we will assume that the contract is between two people.

The three basic elements of every contract are: the *offer*, the *acceptance*, and the *consideration*. *Example*: You show a potential customer a wooden bowl at a craft fair and suggest that she buy it (the offer). The customer says she likes it and wants it (the acceptance). You agree on a price (the consideration). This is the basic framework, but a great many variations can be played on that theme.

TYPES OF CONTRACTS

Contracts may be *express* or *implied*; they may be *oral* or *written*. On this latter point, there are at least two types of contracts that *must* be in writing if they are to be legally enforceable: (1) any contract which, by its terms, cannot be completed in less than one year, and (2) any contract that involves the sale of goods for over $500.

An *express* contract is one in which all the details are spelled out. *Example*: You make a contract with a retail store to deliver two dozen wooden bowls, 12 inches in diameter, made of walnut, to be delivered on or before October 1, at a price of $39.50 per bowl, to be paid for within 30 days of receipt of merchandise.

That's fairly straightforward. If either party fails to live up to any material part of the contract, a breach has occurred; and the other party may withhold performance of his or her obligation until receiving assurance that the breaching party will perform. In the event that no such assurance is forthcoming, the injured party may have a cause of action and can go to court for breach of contract.

If the bowls are delivered on October 15, but the store had advertised a wooden bowl sale for October 1; then time is an important consideration and the store would not be required to accept the late shipment. However, if time is not a material consideration, then the slight delay would probably be considered "substantial performance"; and the store would have to accept the delivery.

Express contracts can be either oral or written; but if you are going to the trouble of expressing contractual terms, you should put your understanding in writing.

Implied contracts need not be very complicated, though they are usually not done in writing. *Example*: You call a supplier to order 100 pounds of clay without making any express statement that you will pay for the clay. The promise to pay is implied in the order and is enforceable when the clay is delivered.

With implied contracts, things can often become a lot stickier. *Example*: An acquaintance asks you to bring over one of your new wall hangings to see how it will look in her living room. She asks if you would leave it with her for a few days. Two months later she still has it, and you overhear her raving to others about how marvelous it looks over the fireplace.

Is there an implied contract to purchase in this arrangement? That may depend on whether you are normally in the business of selling your work, or whether you usually make loans or gifts of your work.

Most contracts that craftspeople enter into in terms of their work involve some aspect of the sale of that work: a direct sale to a customer, a consignment agreement with a dealer who will sell the work, a commission to produce a work.

Let us examine the principles of offer, acceptance, and consideration in several situations for a hypothetical crafts producer, Pat Smith.

Smith is a weaver who also teaches on a part-time basis. Smith has had numerous works accepted in local and regional exhibitions, has won several prizes, and sold a good many woven wall hangings. In a word, Smith is developing quite a reputation as a promising young fiber artist. With this brief background, we will look at the following situations and see whether an enforceable contract comes into existence.

• At a cocktail party, Jones expresses an interest in buying one of Smith's works. "It looks like your weavings will go up in price pretty soon," Jones tells Smith. "I'm going to buy one while I can still afford it."

Is this a contract? If so, what are the terms of the offer—the particular work, the specific price? No, this is not really an offer that Smith can accept. It is nothing more than an opinion or a vague expression of intent.

- Brown offers to pay $400 for one of Smith's wall hangings that had seen in a show several months ago. At the show it was listed at $450, but Smith agrees to accept the lower price.

Is this an enforceable contract? Yes! Brown has offered, in unambiguous terms, to pay a specific amount for a specific work, and Smith has accepted the offer. A binding contract exists.

- One day Jones shows up at Smith's studio and sees a particular wall hanging for which he offers $200. Smith accepts and promises to deliver it the next week, at which time Jones will pay for it. An hour later, Brown shows up. She likes the same wall hanging and offers Smith $300 for it. Can Smith accept the later offer?

No—A contract exists with Jones. An offer was made and accepted. The fact that the object has not yet been delivered or paid for does not make the contract any less binding.

- Green discusses a commission he would like Smith to execute for a particular wall in his office. He offers to pay $600 if the work is satisfactory to him. Green approves preliminary sketches, and Smith completes the work. But, when Smith shows up at Green's office to hang it, Green refuses to accept it because it does not satisfy him.

Green is making the offer in this case, but the offer is conditional upon his satisfaction with the completed work. Smith can only accept the offer by producing something that meets Green's subjective standards—a risky business. There is no enforceable contract for payment until such time as Green indicates that the completed work is satisfactory.

Suppose however, that Green came to Smith's studio and said that the completed work was satisfactory but when Smith delivers it, says it does not look right on his office wall. This is too late for Green to change his mind. The contract became binding at the moment he indicated the work to be satisfactory. If he subsequently refuses to accept it, he would be breaching his contract.

Earlier I mentioned that contracts for goods over $500 must be in writing. Under the Uniform Commercial Code, which governs contracts for the sale of goods, a commission to produce a work is a personal service contract, as distinct from a contract for the sale of a piece already completed. Therefore, the UCC generally does not apply to commissions such as the one described here.

ORAL OR WRITTEN CONTRACTS?

Contracts are enforceable only if they can be proven. All of the hypothetical examples mentioned above could have been oral contracts, but a great deal of detail is often lost in the course of remembering a conversation. The best practice, of course, is to get it in writing. The function of a written contract is not only to provide such proof, but also to make very clear the understanding of the parties regarding the agreement and the terms of the contract.

Some artists and craftspeople are adamant about doing business strictly on the basis of so-called "gentlemen's agreements," particularly with their galleries. The assumption seems to be that the best business relations are those based upon mutual trust. Some artists believe that any agreement other than a gentlemen's agreement belies this trust.

Although there may be some validity to these assumptions, craftspeople would nevertheless be well advised to put all of their oral agreements into writing. Far too many craftspeople have suffered adverse consequences because of their reliance upon the sanctity of oral contracts.

Even in the best of business relationships, it is still possible that one or both parties might forget the terms of an oral agreement. Or, both parties might have quite different perceptions about the precise terms of the agreement. When, however, the agreement is put in writing, there is much less doubt as to the terms of the arrangement, although even a written contract may contain ambiguities if it is not carefully drafted. A written contract generally functions as a safeguard against subsequent misunderstanding or forgetfulness.

Perhaps the principal problem with oral contracts lies in the fact that they cannot always be proven or enforced. Proof of oral contracts typically centers around the conflicting testimony of the parties involved. And if neither party is not able to establish by a preponderance of evidence that his or her version of the contract is the correct one, then the oral contract may be considered nonexistent—as though it had never been made. The same result might ensue if the parties cannot remember the precise terms of the agreement, which is often the case.

WHEN WRITTEN CONTRACTS ARE NECESSARY

Even if an oral contract is established, it may not always be enforceable. There are some agreements which the law requires to be in writing.

An early law that was designed to prevent fraud and perjury, known as the Statute of Frauds, provides that any contract which by its terms cannot be fully performed within one year must be in writing. This rule is narrowly interpreted, so if there is any possibility, no matter how remote, that the contract could be fully performed within one year, the contract need not be reduced to writing.

For example, if a craft artist agrees to submit one large work to a dealer each year for a period of five years, the contract would have to be in writing since by the very terms of the agreement there is no way the contract could be performed within one year. If, on the other hand, the contract called for the artist to deliver five large works within a period of five years, the contract would not have to be in writing under the Statute of Frauds, since it is possible, though perhaps not probable, that the artist could deliver all five works within the first year. The fact that the craft artist does not actually complete performance of the contract within one year is immaterial. So long as complete performance within one year is within the realm of possibility, the contract need not be in writing to be enforceable; it may be oral.

The Statute of Frauds further provides that any contract for the sale of goods of $500 or more is not enforceable unless it has been put in writing and signed by the party against whom the contract is sought to be enforced. The fact that a contract for a price in excess of $500 is not in writing does not void the agreement. The parties are free to perform the oral arrangement; but, if one party refuses to perform, the other will be unable to legally enforce the agreement.

The law defines *goods* as all things that are movable at the time of making the contract except for the money used as payment. There can be little doubt that the vast majority of craft work or craft supplies will be considered goods, so the real question becomes whether a particular contract involves the sale of goods for a price of $500 or more. Although the answer would generally seem to be fairly clear, ambiguities may arise.

For example, if a supplier agrees to provide the craftsperson with all of his or her craft supply needs for the coming month, how is the price to be determined? Or if the artist sells a number of works to a dealer where the total purchase price exceeds $500, but the price of the individual works is less than $500, which price governs? In light of such ambiguities it would seem that the safer course would be to put all oral contracts in writing.

NO-COST WRITTEN AGREEMENTS

At this point, craftspeople might object by asserting that they do not have the time, energy or patience to draft contracts. After all, the business of the artist is the creation of art, not the formulation of written contracts steeped in legal jargon.

Fortunately, the craftsperson will not always be required to do this, since the art supplier or retailer may be willing to draft a contract satisfactory to the artist. However, be wary of signing any form contracts—they will almost invariably be one-sided, with all terms drafted in favor of whomever paid to have them drafted.

As a second alternative, the artist could employ an attorney to draft the contracts. This may only be worthwhile where the contract involves a substantial transaction. With respect to smaller transactions, the legal fees may be much larger than the benefits derived from having a written contract.

The Uniform Commercial Code, a compilation of commercial laws enacted in every state except Louisiana, provides craftspeople with a third and perhaps the best alternative. They need not actually draft a contract nor rely on anyone else (a supplier, art dealer or attorney) to do so. The UCC provides that where both parties are merchants and one party sends to the other a written confirmation of an oral contract within a reasonable time after that contract has been made, and the recipient does not object to the confirming memorandum within ten days of its receipt, then the contract will be deemed enforceable.

A *merchant* is defined as any person who normally deals in goods of the kind sold or who by his occupation represents himself as having knowledge or skill peculiar to the practices or goods involved in the transaction. Thus, professional craftspeople and craft dealers will be deemed merchants. Even an amateur artist will be considered a merchant since adopting the designation *artist* or *potter* or *weaver* should be deemed as representing oneself as having special knowledge or skill in the field. The rule will, therefore, apply to most oral contracts the artist may make.

It should be emphasized that the sole effect of the confirming memorandum is that neither party can use the Statute of Frauds as a defense, assuming that the recipient fails to object within ten days after receipt. The party sending the confirming memorandum still must prove that an oral contract was, in fact, made prior to or at the same time as the written confirmation. Once such proof is offered, neither party can raise the Statute of Frauds to avoid enforcement of agreement.

The advantage of the confirming memorandum over a written contract lies in the fact that the confirming memorandum can be used without the active participation of the other contracting party. It would suffice, for example, to simply state: "This memorandum is to confirm our oral agreement."

Since the artist would still have to prove the terms of that agreement, it would be useful to provide a bit more detail in the confirming memorandum, such as the subject of the contract, the date it was made and the price or other consideration to be paid. Thus, the artist might draft something like the following:

This memorandum is to confirm our oral agreement made on July 3, 1991, pursuant to which (artist) agreed to deliver to (dealer) on or before September 19, 1991, five pieces of pottery for the purchase price of $600.

The advantages of providing some detail in the confirming memorandum are twofold. First, in the event of a dispute, the craftsperson could introduce the memorandum as proof of the terms of the oral agreement. Second, the recipient of the memorandum will be precluded from offering any proof regarding the terms of the oral contract that contradicts the terms contained in the memorandum. The recipient or, for that matter, the party sending the memorandum can only introduce proof regarding the terms of the oral contract that are consistent with the terms, if any, found in the memorandum. Thus, the dealer in the above example would be precluded from claiming that the contract called for delivery of six pieces of pottery because the quantity was stated and not objected to.

On the other hand, a dealer would be permitted to testify that the oral contract required the potter to package the pottery in a specific way since this testimony would not be inconsistent with the terms stated in the memorandum.

One party to a contract can prevent the other from adding or inventing terms that are not spelled out in the confirming memorandum by ending the memorandum with a clause requiring all other provisions to be contained in a written and signed document. Such a clause might read:

This is the entire agreement between the parties and no modification, alteration, or additional terms shall be enforceable unless in writing and signed by both parties.

To summarize, craftspeople should not rely on oral contracts alone since they offer little protection in the event of a dispute. The best protection is afforded by a written contract. It is a truism that oral contracts are not worth the paper on which they are written. If drafting a complete written contract proves too burdensome or costly, the craftsmaker should at least submit a memorandum in confirmation of his or her oral contracts. This at least overcomes the initial barrier raised by the Statute of Frauds. Moreover, by recounting the terms in the memorandum, the craftsperson is in a much better position later on to prove the oral contract.

SUMMARY OF ESSENTIALS TO PUT IN WRITING

A contract rarely need be—or should be—a long, complicated document written in legal jargon designed to provide a handsome income to lawyers. Indeed, a contract should be written in simple language that both parties can understand, and should spell out the terms of the agreement.

The contract would include: (1) the date of the agreement; (2) identification of the two parties, the buyer and seller in the case of craftwork; (3) description of the work being sold; (4) price or other consideration; and (5) the signatures of the parties.

To supplement these basics, the agreement should spell out whatever other terms might be applicable: pricing arrangements, payment schedules, insurance coverage, consignment details, and so forth.

Finally, it should be noted that a written document that leaves out essential terms of the contract presents many of the same problems of proof and ambiguity as an oral contract. Con-

tract terms should be well conceived, clearly drafted, "conspicuous" (i.e., not in tiny print that is difficult to read), and in
plain English so everyone understands what the terms of the
contract are.

4

CONSIGNMENT

One of the more difficult aspects of being a craftsperson is selling your work. Many craftworkers find this part of their profession to be a bit too mundane to warrant much time or consideration, but the fact remains that craftworkers must, generally, sell their work if they are to survive and devote significant amounts of time to the business of creating. Those craftspersons who are unable or unwilling to market their works are usually compelled to seek other employment, which detracts from the time they could spend as professional craftmakers.

There are three basic ways by which craftspeople sell their work: (1) *direct sales*, as at craft shows or in their own retail shops; (2) *wholesale* to department stores, boutiques, museum shops and the like; and (3) *consignment*, usually to galleries, but often to other retail outlets as well. Many craftspeople sell their work via a combination of all three methods.

Working on large commissions or selling through agents is another sales method, but this generally applies only to the more successful or prolific craftspeople.

Direct selling and wholesaling are fairly matter-of-fact situations, at least as far as the legal ramifications are concerned. One party sells, the other party buys, and money changes hands at the time the goods are transferred (or shortly thereafter). When the goods leave the seller's possession, they become the property of the buyer.

Consignment selling can be quite a bit more complicated. Under a typical consignment arrangement, the craftsperson (the *consignor*) delivers his or her work to a gallery or other dealer (the *consignee*). The consignee does not make an outright purchase of the work but, rather, agrees to remit to the consignor the proceeds from sales less the consignment commission as the sales are made. Generally, the consignee is under no obligation to sell the goods and may return them to the consignor at any time.

ADVANTAGES OF CONSIGNMENT

Although it may not be immediately obvious, the consignment arrangement can be beneficial to both the craftworker and gallery alike. For the gallery, consignments eliminate much of the financial risks of carrying works of questionable market appeal. If the work does not sell, or sells poorly, the gallery will generally not lose much money since it has made no direct investment by purchasing the pieces. The gallery only loses to the extent that the display space filled by the consigned work could have been filled by other pieces having greater sales potential, along with whatever amount of money was expended on advertising, overhead, etc.

The advantage to the craftworker is that consignment provides an opportunity to get a product into retail outlets where it might not otherwise be accepted. This is particularly true for the work of unknown craftspeople who find that this is often the only way they can prove that their work will sell. Another advantage is that the craftworker generally gets a larger share of the retail selling price (around 60 percent in consignment versus 50 percent in wholesaling—though that is changing, and consignment percentages are getting closer and closer to the 50 percent wholesale arrangement).

DISADVANTAGES OF CONSIGNMENT

But there are several deterrents which often make craftspeople reluctant to engage in consignment selling. After all, it is the craftsperson who takes most of the risks in such arrangements. Some of the questions that are bound to occur are: How promptly does the consignee pay after the work is sold? Is the work insured while it is on the consignee's premises? Will unsold work be returned in good condition? And how much paperwork and record keeping will be involved?

Other deterrents to the consignment arrangement are more complicated. What happens, for example, if a craftsperson puts his or her work in a gallery on consignment and the gallery subsequently goes bankrupt? Or, what if the gallery fails to pay debts to a creditor who has a security interest in the gallery's assets? Would the security interest cover the consigned work? The resolution of these questions depends upon a determination of which party, the craftworker on the one hand or the creditor or bankruptcy trustee on the other, has priority over the consigned work. There is no question that all of these parties may have valid claims to the work; the question is, rather, whose claims are to be given first priority.

YOUR SITUATION IN A GALLERY BANKRUPTCY

Before the enactment of the uniform state law called the Uniform Commercial Code (UCC), the craftmaker as a consignor would generally prevail over the consignee/gallery's creditors or the consignee's trustee in bankruptcy with respect to the consigned work. Moreover, the craftworker would prevail even if there were no record of the consignment to give creditors or a trustee in bankruptcy notice of the consignment's existence. In effect, the craftsperson held a secret lien on the consigned work that was given priority over all other liens.

The UCC has been adopted in all states, except Louisiana

which has adopted only parts of the UCC. For our purposes, however, Louisiana law is in line with the discussion that follows.

Thus, Article 2 of the UCC provides that where a craftsperson delivers work to a business dealing in goods of that kind, such as a gallery, the craftworker will not have priority over the claims of creditors or a trustee in bankruptcy unless the craftworker does one of three things:

(1) Complies with the applicable state law providing that the consignor's interest be evidenced by a sign on the goods; or

(2) Establishes in court that the consignee is known by his or her creditors to be substantially engaged in selling goods under consignment; or

(3) Complies with the filing requirements in Article 9 of the UCC.

As to the first option, most states do not have sign laws. Even in those states that do, the consignor should not rely on the consignee to place and maintain a sign on the goods indicating that they have been consigned since it may not be in the interests of the consignee to do so. For example, a gallery would generally be in a much better position to obtain loans if a lending institution was led to believe that all of the work in the gallery was owned outright as opposed to being consigned.

Additionally, the consignor should not expect to prevail under the second option since it will generally be difficult to prove that the consignee was known by the creditors to be substantially engaged in the business of selling consigned goods. This problem is made somewhat easier for the craftworker by the fact that many galleries in the United States sell their works on consignment. Nevertheless, the craftworker would be ill-advised to rely exclusively on this option as a means of protecting his or her work. Merely pointing to customary practices in the crafts world may not be sufficient to meet the craftperson's burden of proof.

This leaves the third option. As a general rule, the craftworker can best protect his or her consigned work by complying with the filing provisions contained in Article 9 of the UCC. The purpose of the Article 9 filing requirement is simply to give notice to interested parties that certain property is subject to outstanding interests. The filing requirement gives notice to creditors, lending institutions and the like that the work within the gallery is subject to a consignment agreement between the gallery and the craftperson.

This process is a complicated, time-consuming exercise that requires the filing of financing statements with the Secretary of State in every state where the consigned work is located, paying filing fees each time, giving notice to the consignee's creditors, and several other requirements.

There has been considerable debate as to whether the UCC provisions adequately safeguard the craftworker's interests under consignment arrangements. As an initial consideration, there is the problem that craftspeople may not even be aware that the protection exists. Unlike consignors in other fields, artists and craftspeople are not always sophisticated in the ways of business and law.

Moreover, even if the craftworker knows the protection exists, he or she may be unable or unwilling to learn how that protection can be secured. Or, in terms of complying with the filing requirements of Article 9, many craftspeople who know what is needed may find that approach too complex and bothersome.

SPECIFIC LAWS COVERING CONSIGNMENT

As a result of these problems and others, many states have enacted special artist-gallery consignment laws. The first of these was enacted by New York in 1966. Subsequently, similar legislation was passed in twenty-eight other states: Alaska, Arizona, Arkansas, California, Colorado, Connecticut, Florida, Idaho, Illinois, Iowa, Kentucky, Maryland, Massachusetts, Michigan, Minnesota, Missouri, Montana, New Hampshire, New Jersey, New Mexico, North Carolina, Ohio, Oregon, Pennsylvania,

Tennessee, Texas, Washington and Wisconsin. Other states are considering such laws, largely in response to pressures from artists and arts organizations.

Although each state has enacted a unique version, the basic provisions of artist-gallery consignment laws are essentially the same. Most statutes provide that any works of art delivered to any art dealer are presumed to be delivered under a consignment arrangement unless the artist has been paid in full on or before delivery. Thus, the majority of transactions between artists and various art dealers will be deemed consignments for purposes of these statutes.

In addition, most artist-gallery consignment statutes provide that the art dealer hold all consigned artwork, as well as the proceeds derived from the sale of the artwork, in trust for the benefit of the artist. This basically means that the art dealer will be solely responsible for any loss, theft or damage to the consigned artwork that could have been avoided had the art dealer exercised the utmost care and caution. Many statutes impose strict liability upon the dealer for loss or damage, i.e., the art dealer will be liable even though such loss or damage could not have been avoided by the utmost care and caution.

Several of the new laws require the artist and the dealer to enter into a written agreement containing at least the following information: the value of the artwork, the minimum price for which it can be sold, and the percentage to be paid to the dealer. Additional issues that may be addressed include: the duration of the consignment relationship, who assumes the costs for shipping and storage, the payment schedule for the craftsperson, and the extent and nature of marketing and promotion done by the dealer. The protective provisions of consignment legislation typically cannot be waived. Therefore, any attempt to avoid these provisions by contract are prohibited by the laws themselves.

Finally, and perhaps most importantly, nearly all of these statutes provide that the consigned artwork is protected against claims asserted by the art dealer's creditors, including the trustee in bankruptcy. Thus, at least one effect of the consignment legislation is to provide artists with similar protection to that afforded by Article 9 of the UCC without requiring the artist to take any steps to procure that protection.

(See the section on Gallery Bankruptcy [Chapter 11, on Getting Paid] for additional information.)

CRAFT WORKS: COVERED OR NOT?

Although art consignment legislation would seem to solve many of the practical problems with consignments, the craftsperson as artist should review how the applicable legislation, if any, defines the terms *art dealer* and *artwork*. Fortunately, for the craftsperson, art dealer has been broadly defined by nearly all states as being any person engaged in the business of selling artwork other than a person exclusively engaged in selling goods at public auction. On the other hand, artwork has sometimes been given a rather narrow definition. A few statutes have defined artwork as encompassing only the traditional areas of fine art, such as painting, sculpture, drawing and the like. This means that under some consignment statutes, the product of the craftsperson may not be deemed to be within the purview of the statutory protection. Most statutes expressly include craft works such as those made of clay, fiber, wood, metal, plastic or glass as being within the definition of a work of art protected by the legislation.

Whether the exclusion of crafts from some consignment legislation was merely an oversight or a reflection of the long-standing, though unwarranted, notion that crafts are somehow inferior to the traditional fine arts is not clear. In any event, people engaged in the various crafts would do well to form or support cohesive lobbying organizations and thereby strengthen their power with state legislators. If enough pressure were placed upon legislators, existing statutes could be amended to include crafts within their protection and new legislation could be drafted correctly to include crafts within the scope of protected works.

EXCLUSIVITY

Craftspeople should carefully consider the important issue of exclusivity when entering into a consignment arrangement. There are two types of exclusivity: exclusive agency and exclusive power to sell. If the dealer is the exclusive agent of the craftsperson, the craftsperson can sell works independently and not be liable to the dealer for a commission. If the exclusivity arrangement is for the power to sell, the craftsperson who independently sells works is liable to the dealer for a commission, or may be in breach of their contract.

In addition to outright sales, there is a question about exclusivity as applied to "bartering" situations. If you, as craftmaker, exchange your vase for the use of a condominium, is your exclusive agent, the dealer, entitled to a commission? Art dealers usually interpret exclusive arrangements broadly, but the craftsperson's interpretation may be quite different. Unless the craftsperson is a powerhouse in the field, there is likely to be a disparity in bargaining power between the craftsperson and the dealer. A craftsperson may be intimidated into agreeing to an exclusive arrangement.

Exclusivity carries both positive and negative aspects. The gallery dealer benefits by being the only agent for the craftmaker, thereby generating business, particularly if the craftmaker is well-known and appreciated. In return, the dealer believes that the craftmaker benefits because the gallery promotes the artist as well as his or her works. Craftmakers, on the other hand, may see an exclusive arrangement as too restrictive. The craftmaker is a separate entity from the created works. An exclusive arrangement that binds the two together reduces the freedom of the craftmaker to pursue other avenues. Also, if minimum sales are not guaranteed, the craftmaker is not assured a return. He or she, however, may not go outside of the arrangement to promote his or her works.

Some of the factors that you, as a craftworker, should consider when faced with the decision of entering into an exclusivity contract are: Is there direct competition between the galleries you are interested in dealing with; is the gallery owner willing to guarantee a minimum amount in sales; and is your line diverse enough to be shown in more than one gallery in a given geographic area.

As a craftworker, you should carefully consider the pluses and minuses of an exclusive dealer arrangement. Marketing your work is the key.

5

WORKING AT HOME

It is extremely common for artists and craftspeople to have studios or workshops in a home or garage. This is true for a variety of reasons, including the desire to be able to work whenever one has the urge, regardless of the hour. The most important reason, though, is probably one of economics. The cost of renting a separate studio or workshop can be prohibitive; not too many artists or craftspeople are willing or able to pay it. Others, of course, choose to work at home because it enables them to juggle work and family obligations.

The problems raised by the multiple use of a dwelling can be divided into two basic areas: namely, whether the income tax laws recognize the realities of the arts and crafts world, and whether local zoning regulations allow you legally to work and live in the same place.

TAX CONSIDERATIONS

First, let us examine whether and how artists and craftspeople can obtain tax deductions for the use of their homes in their businesses.

Before 1976, an artist or craftsperson could deduct that portion of household expenses which could reasonably be allocated to professional work. In 1976, Congress added Section 280A to the Internal Revenue Code. This law generally disallows any deduction for the use of one's personal residence in any business. It applies not only to the building in which the taxpayer lives, but also to any structure attached to the house or on the property. There are, however, limited exceptions to the law.

EXCLUSIVE AND REGULAR USE

Some artists and craftspeople may be able to satisfy one or more of the exceptions to this rule. The first exception is for any portion of the residence used *exclusively* and *on a regular basis* as the artist's or craftsperson's *principal place of business* or to meet clients or customers.

The qualifications for this exception are strictly construed by the IRS and the courts. The requirement of exclusivity means that the taxpayer may not mix personal use and business use. In other words, a taxpayer may not deduct expenses for a studio if it is also used as a storeroom for personal belongings, a laundry room, or the like.

There has been a recent liberalization of this rule in parts of the country where courts have ruled that a studio can exist in a room that has a non-business use. Under proposed Regulation 1.280A-2(g)(1), the IRS will accept any "separately identifiable" area that is exclusively used for a home office. It need not be a separate room, nor permanently partitioned.

The requirement regarding regularity means that the use of the room may not be merely incidental or occasional. Obviously, there is a gray area between regular and occasional. Perhaps some artists or craftspeople can use this rule as an inducement to overcome temporary bouts of laziness or boredom. For if you are an artist or craftmaker and plan to deduct any expenses for your studio, you must keep working to satisfy the regularity test.

The "focal point" test is used to determine the principal place of business. The test focuses on the place where services are performed and income is generated. Key elements are: (1) the amount of income derived from the business done there; (2) the amount of time spent there; and (3) the nature of the facility.

The Tax Court has, on one occasion, strayed from the focal point test. The court determined that a home office deduction, while not able to meet the principal place of business test was, nevertheless, *essential* to the taxpayer's business. The deduction was allowed; however, it raised the ire of the IRS. It would not be prudent for a craftperson to rely on this liberal interpretation until it is more firmly entrenched.

IRS Regulation 1.280A-2(b) allows a taxpayer to have a different principal place of business for each trade or business in which that person is engaged. Thus, it is now possible, for example, for a teacher, whose principal place of business (judging by income and time spent) is the school, to also run a sideline business of making and selling craft objects out of the home and to claim the home studio as the principal place of business for the craft enterprise.

When an artist or craftsperson is employed by another in his or her professional capacity as an artist or craftsperson, a deduction for the home studio is more difficult to justify. In addition to fulfilling the tests outlined above, the employee's use of the home studio must be "for the convenience of his employer." This test would not be met if the employer provides a studio for his employees.

When the studio is in a structure separate from the principal residence, the requirements for deductibility are less stringent. The structure must be used exclusively and on a regular basis, just as a studio in the home itself. However, when the studio is in a separate structure, the studio need only be used "in connection with" the artistic business, not as the principal place of business.

When artists or craftspeople use a portion of their homes for storage purposes, the requirements for deductibility are also less stringent. The dwelling must be the sole fixed location of the business and must be used on a regular basis for the storage of the artist's or craftsperson's works. The entire room used for storage need not be used exclusively for business, but there must be a "separately identifiable space suitable for storage" of the artist's or craftsperson's works.

ARE THE DEDUCTIONS WORTHWHILE?

If an artist or craftsperson meets one of the tests outlined above, the next question is what tax benefits can result. After close analysis, the answer is frequently: "Not very many." An *allocable portion* of mortgage interest and property taxes can be deducted against the business, but these would be deductible anyway if the taxpayer itemizes. The advantage of deducting them against the business is that this reduces the business profit that is subject to self-employment taxes.

Of course, a taxpayer who rents a house and otherwise qualifies for the deductions may deduct a portion of the rent that would not otherwise be tax deductible. The primary tax advantage comes from a deduction of an allocable portion of repairs, utility bills and depreciation. These would not otherwise be deductible.

To arrive at the allocable portion, take the square footage of the space used for the business and divide that by the total square footage of the house. Multiply this fraction by the sum of your mortgage interest, property taxes, etc., for the amount to be deducted from the business. How to determine the amount of allowable depreciation is too complex to discuss here.

The total amount that can be deducted for a studio or storage place in the home is artificially limited. To determine the amount that can be deducted, take the total amount of money earned in the business and subtract the business deductions allowed for supplies, salaries, etc., as well as the allocable portion of mortgage interest and property taxes. The remainder is the maximum amount that you can deduct for the allocable portion of repairs, utilities and depreciation. In other words, your total business deductions in this situation cannot be greater than your total business income.

If this number is negative, there is no deduction allowed. Taxpayers are now allowed to carry over to the next year any deductions for home office use that are not allowed because of the gross income limit. The limit, of course, applies each year.

The IRS has also determined that a taxpayer cannot deduct any charges, including excise and sales taxes, that are paid to obtain phone service for the *first* residential phone line. This means that a taxpayer with a single phone line cannot deduct any charges that could otherwise be allocable to business use.

Besides the obvious complexity of the rules and the mathematics, there are several other factors that limit the benefit of taking a deduction for a studio in the home. One of these is the partial loss of the *nonrecognition of gain* (tax deferred) treatment that is otherwise allowed when a taxpayer sells a personal residence. Ordinarily, when someone sells a personal residence for a profit, the tax on the gain is deferred if the seller purchases another personal residence of at least the same value within two years. Most of the tax on this gain is never paid during the taxpayer's lifetime since it is unusual to sell one's personal residence and not purchase another one.

This deferral of gain, however, is not allowed to the extent that the house was used in the business. This means that the taxpayer must pay tax on the allocable portion of the gain from the sale, including tax on any recapture of accelerated depreciation he or she has taken in prior years.

Example: If you have been claiming 20 percent of your home as a business deduction, when you sell the home you will enjoy a tax deferral on only 80 percent of the profit. The other 20 percent will be subject to tax because that 20 percent represents the sale of a business asset. In essence, for the price of a current deduction you may be converting what is essentially a nonrecognition, or tax-deferred, asset into a trade or business property.

However, there is one important exception that can work to your advantage. In Revenue Ruling 82-26, the IRS ruled that *if you stop qualifying* for the home office/studio tax deduction for at least one year before you sell the house, you are entitled to the entire gain as *rollover*, no matter how long you had taken the deduction in prior years.

The word *qualifying* in that ruling has a very important meaning. It does not mean only that you stop taking the business deduction for one year. It means that you physically move the business out of your home so that it no longer qualifies as a home business expense, whether you take it as a tax deduction or not. The same ruling applies to the one-time tax exemption of up to $125,000 on the sale of a home by persons over age 55. If you plan to sell anytime soon, check all this out with an accountant. A little planning might save you a great deal of money.

Another negative factor is that, by deducting for a studio in the home, the taxpayer in effect puts a red flag on his or her tax return. Obviously, when the tax return expressly asks whether expenses are being deducted for an office in the home, the question is not being asked for purely academic reasons. Although only the IRS knows how much the answer to this question affects someone's chances of being audited, there is little doubt that a "yes" answer does increase the likelihood of an audit.

Given this increased possibility of audit, it does not pay to deduct for a studio in the home in doubtful situations. Taxpayers who lose the deduction must pay back taxes plus interest or fight in court. One unfortunate taxpayer not only lost the deduction on a technicality, but also lost the rollover treatment on the sale of his home because the court found that the business-use limitation, or rollover, was broader than the section that allows deductions for business use.

If you believe that your home studio or workshop could qualify for the business deduction, you would be well-advised to consult with a competent tax expert who can assist in calculating the deduction.

LEGAL CONSIDERATIONS

Let us turn now to some of the legal considerations involved in living and working in the same space. Local zoning ordinances and federal labor regulations can all have an effect on such a set-up. In some instances this may make working at home less attractive than it might otherwise seem. In evaluating the feasibility of working at home, craftspeople will need to consider the effects of several different laws.

LOCAL ZONING RESTRICTIONS

For the craftsperson who wants to live and work in the same space, local zoning ordinances can be a significant factor. Some city and county ordinances flatly prohibit using the same space as a business and a dwelling. In some commercially zoned areas where craftspeople can rent low-cost lofts and studios, it is illegal to maintain a residence in the same space. In residential areas, the craftsperson may have to comply with regulations that require permits and restrict the size and use of the studio.

Municipal and county ordinances vary, and the craftmaker should, therefore, check with the appropriate local government agency or agencies to determine specific requirements. The fire department, for example, will undoubtedly have to approve the use of a kiln.

For the craftsperson who wants to maintain a studio or workshop in the garage or basement of a residence, several types of restrictions may apply. The space devoted to the craft activity may be limited to a certain number of square feet; outbuildings may or may not be allowed. The type of equipment used may also be restricted. Noise, smoke and odor restrictions may apply and the craftsperson may have to obtain approval from all or some of the neighbors. If remodeling is contemplated, building codes must, of course, also be considered.

The craftsperson also may have to obtain a home occupation permit or, in many areas, a business license. The application fee for either of these will normally be a flat fee or a percentage of annual receipts from the activity. Depending upon the success of the business, this can be a substantial expense. In addition, the craftmaker's homeowner or renter insurance policy may contain some restrictions on commercial activity. The craftsperson should, therefore, contact the insurance broker to find out whether such limitations exist and what can be done to deal with them.

In commercially zoned areas, craftspeople may have more flexibility in the types of activities they conduct, particularly if the craft produces noise or odors that would be offensive to others in a residentially zoned location. But, if the craftmaker also wishes to use the work space for eating and sleeping, zoning ordinances may prohibit such use.

Some cities have recognized the hardships these zoning ordinances create for artists and craftspeople. In New York City, for example, a municipal dwelling law was enacted exempting artists and their families from restrictions against living and working in the same apartment unit. The State of California also has enacted legislation that grants local municipalities the right to adopt zoning ordinances that would accommodate artists who live in industrially or commercially zoned areas.

While these laws have solved the immediate problem of artists and craftspeople living and working in the same location, new problems were created. Once it became possible for artists to live and work in the SoHo district of New York City, for example, the area became a magnet for galleries, boutiques, restaurants and tourists. Many artists remain, but many had to move, having been forced out by skyrocketing rents and prices.

Before SoHo became fashionable, no new industry could be enticed into the area. Consequently, landlords were pleased to have artists leasing their commercial property. Once development caught on, however, buildings changed hands more often, and artists and craftspeople who had invested substantial sums in their lofts found that their commercial leases afforded them little protection from substantial, unanticipated increases in rent.

However, a 1979 New York case, *Mandel v. Pitkowsky*, may provide residential loft tenants with some degree of security. Pitkowsky and sculptor Ulrich Niemeyer had rented commercial quarters for ten years. Their lease limited their occupancy to an artist's studio. Nevertheless, their landlord encouraged them to convert the studio into their residence. Both sides were happy to abide by this illegal arrangement, apparently secure in the knowledge that the city was not diligently inspecting these properties. When the lease expired, however, the landlord demanded a threefold increase in the rent. The landlord claimed that because the property was commercial rather than residential, it was not subject to the city's rent-stabilization laws. The court did not agree: the landlord's express approval of the tenants' ten-year residency converted the studio into a *de facto* multiple dwelling.

FEDERAL REGULATIONS

Another type of regulation that can and has adversely affected craftspeople who want to work at home are federal laws that inhibit cottage industries. For almost forty years, the U.S. Department of Labor actively enforced a 1943 regulation prohibiting individuals from producing six categories of crafts in their homes: embroidery, women's apparel, gloves and mittens, buttons and buckles, jewelry, and handkerchiefs. The Department was primarily concerned with violations of the minimum wage provisions of the Fair Labor Standards Act which requires employers to pay their employees no less than a set minimum hourly wage ($4.35 as of April 1, 1991). Overtime pay, at one-and-one-half times the hourly rate, is mandated for hours worked over forty per week.

In 1982 the Department repealed the prohibition on knitted outerwear; however, it faced bitter union opposition. Eight years later, in 1989, the prohibitions on the remaining five categories were lifted although, in the case of jewelry, the prohibition was lifted only for nonhazardous jewelry work. This greatly decreases the difficulties that have faced home craftworkers in the past.

But, what the Department has lifted, it can reimpose if "significant wage or other violations" are found among homeworkers. Craftspeople should be aware that these or similar regulations may reappear.

6

KEEPING TAXES LOW

Although artists and craftspeople rarely think of themselves as being involved in the world of commerce, the IRS treats the professional craftworker like anyone else in business. Thus, the craftsperson has many of the same tax concerns as any other businessperson. In addition, most craftspeople have some special tax problems.

First, the professional craftsperson generally does not work for a fixed wage or salary. As a result, income can fluctuate radically from one tax year to the next. Second, many tax rules designed to facilitate investment are not useful to the craftsperson. Craftspeople can, however, benefit from certain provisions of the Internal Revenue Code to reduce their tax liability. In this chapter I will cover income-tax issues only.

RECORDKEEPING

In order to take advantage of all the tax laws that are favorable to you, it is imperative that you keep good business records. The Internal Revenue Service does not require that you keep any particular type of records. It will be satisfied so long as your recordkeeping clearly reflects your income and is consistent over time so that accurate comparisons from year to year can be made when evaluating your income.

The first step to keeping business records that will allow you to maximize your deductions is to open a business checking account. Try to pay all your business expenses by check. Be sure to fill in the amount, date, and reason for each check on the stub. If the check was written for an expense related to a particular client or job, be sure to put the client's name or a job number on both the check and the stub. Finally, keep all of your cancelled checks.

Second, you should file for a taxpayer identification number. In most states and in some cities, the sale of craftwork is considered a business subject to sales tax. You will need to contact your state and city sales tax bureaus to find out their requirements. Usually, a bureau will issue you a taxpayer identification number after you fill out some forms. Then you, as a manufacturer, can buy certain equipment and supplies without paying the sales tax. However, you will later have to act as an agent of the state, collecting sales tax from your customers and paying it to the state. Be aware that even if you do not collect the sales tax from your customers, you will be liable for paying it.

Third, keep an expense diary which is similar in form to a date book. Use this expense diary on a daily basis, noting all cash outlays such as business-related cab fares, tolls, tips, and emergency supplies as they occur. This will satisfy the IRS requirement that, for expenses over $25, you have both a receipt and good evidence of the business purpose of an expense listed in a logical way (such as in a diary).

INCOME SPREADING

There are two principal ways of reducing tax liability. First, craftspeople can spread their taxable income (and thus reduce tax liability) by using several provisions in the tax code. Second, significant deductions are available to craftspeople.

One strategy for craftworkers in high tax brackets is to divert some of their income directly to members of their immediate family who are in lower tax brackets by hiring them as employees. Putting dependent children on the payroll can result in tax savings for professional craftspeople in a higher tax bracket because they can deduct the salaries as a business expense. It should be noted, however, that wages earned by children between the ages of 18 and 21 who work in their parents' business are subject to social security payroll taxes.

Your child can earn an amount equivalent to the standard deduction plus the personal exemption without incurring any income tax liability. The personal exemption and standard deduction (filing singly) for 1990 were $2,050 and $3,250, respectively, with each being subject to adjustment for inflation in subsequent years. The Internal Revenue Code does not allow a child to claim a personal exemption if he or she can be claimed by the parent(s), as for example, when the child is a full-time student for whom the parent provides more than half of his or her support. There are also some restrictions on placing children on the payroll:

(1) The salary must be reasonable in relation to the child's age and work performed;
(2) The work must be necessary to the business; and
(3) The child must actually do the work.

A second method of transferring income to family members is to create a family partnership. Each partner is entitled to receive an equal share of the overall income unless the partnership agreement provides otherwise. The income is taxed as personal income to each partner. Thus, the craftsperson with a family partnership can break up and divert income to the family members, where it will be taxed according to their respective tax brackets. The revision in the tax law creates only three tax brackets; however, there is still a chance for considerable savings. The income received by children may be taxed at significantly lower rates. This results in more income reaching the family than if it had all been received solely by the craftsperson, who would be, presumably, in a higher tax bracket than the children. But, the Internal Revenue Code of 1986 stipulates that if a child is under 14 and receives unearned income from the partnership, any amount over $500 will be taxed at the parent's highest marginal rate. This provision actually allows the child to receive up to $1,000 before unearned income is taxed at the parent's rate. (The child has a personal exemption of $500 added to the $500 limit imposed by the provision.) A family partnership is not necessary if the partners are husband and wife because the tax advantage is inherent in filing a joint return.

Although the IRS allows family partnerships, it may subject them to close scrutiny to ensure that the partnership is not a sham. Persons designated as partners must have control consistent with that status. In the case of a minor, that control can be exercised by a fiduciary, or the minor can be a limited partner.

Unless the partnership capital is a substantial income-producing factor and partners are reasonably compensated for services performed on the partnership's behalf, the IRS may forbid the shift in income by relying on the Code section that deals with distribution of partners' shares and family partnerships. This section also provides that a person owning a capital interest in a family partnership will be considered a partner for tax purposes, even if he or she received the capital interest as a gift. Such a gift must be genuine and should not be revocable.

INCORPORATING A FAMILY

In the past, some families incorporated in order to take advantage of the then more favorable corporate tax rates. If the IRS questioned the motivation for such incorporation, the courts examined the intent of the family members. If the sole purpose of incorporating was tax avoidance, the scheme was disallowed.

The Tax Reform Act of 1986 reduced the individual income tax rates so that, for most taxpayers, the rates are substantially in line with or lower than the tax imposed on corporations. The problem of double taxation on dividends as explained in Chapter 1 also exists. It seems, therefore, less advantageous to incorporate. However, one advantage of incorporating as a traditional "C" corporation is that the cost of medical, dental and reimbursement plans for the principals can be paid for using pre-tax dollars. Also, you can obtain the limited liability advantages discussed in Chapter 1.

A craftsperson may also elect to incorporate and be taxed as an "S" corporation. This enables the corporation to insulate the craftsperson from personal liability while permitting the business to be taxed as if it were individually owned.

If the craftsperson employs a spouse and children, their salaries are considered business deductions and reduce the craftsperson's taxable income. When the spouse and children are given shares of stock and made owners of the corporation, all the benefits discussed in the preceding section on partnerships are available. Note, however, that losses from passive investment, such as stock ownership, may be used only to offset earnings from passive investments and are not deductible against ordinary income. As for the unearned income received from the corporation by a child under 14, the same rule applies as in a family partnership; amounts over $500 are taxed at the parent's rate.

If the craftsperson, as employee of the "S" corporation, is paid a nominal salary and significant dividends are declared, this dividend income is not subject to social security or withholding taxes. However, the IRS has been known to reclassify these dividends as *constructive wages*, thus making the corporation liable for these taxes. A craftsperson should carefully consider the advantages and disadvantages of forming a family partnership or incorporating in light of his or her specific situation and needs.

There is a further advantage to incorporating, whether as a "C" or "S" corporation. The corporation and a shareholder can enter into a contract that obligates the corporation to purchase the shareholder's stock when the shareholder dies. The corporation can then purchase an insurance policy on the life of the shareholder in order to provide funds for the stock purchase.

This life insurance policy is a business expense and, as such, the cost of the insurance premium is likely to be deductible.

BUSINESS DEDUCTIONS

Until now, we have been discussing the ways craftspeople can spread their taxable income. Another means of reducing tax liability involves making use of deductions. Craftspeople may deduct their business expenses and thereby significantly reduce taxable income. However, as with other artists, they must be able to establish that they are engaged in a trade or business — not merely a personal hobby. A hobbyist or dilettante is not entitled to trade or business deductions. You must keep full and accurate records. Receipts are a necessity. Furthermore, it is best to have a separate checking account and a complete set of books for all of the activities of your trade or business.

Tax laws presume that a craftsperson is engaged in a business or trade, as opposed to a hobby, if a net profit results from the activity in question during three out of five consecutive years, ending with the tax year in question. If the craftworker has not had three profitable years in the last five as a craftsperson, the IRS may contend that he or she is merely indulging in a hobby, in which case a *profit motive* will have to be proven in order to claim business expenses. Proof of profit motive does not require the person to prove that there was some chance a profit would be made; it only requires proof that the person intended to make a profit.

The Treasury Department Regulations call for an objective standard on the profit-motive issue, so statements of the craftsperson as to intent will not suffice as proof. The regulation lists nine factors to be used in determining profit motive; however, this list is not all-inclusive:

- How the taxpayer carries on the activity (i.e., effective business routines and bookkeeping procedures).
- The expertise of the taxpayer or the taxpayer's advisors (e.g., study in a related area, awards, prior sales or exhibitions, crit-

ical recognition, membership in professional organizations, etc.).

• The time and effort spent on the activity (at least several hours a day, preferably on a regular basis).

• Expectation that business assets will increase in value (a factor of little relevance to the craftsperson).

• The success of the taxpayer in similar or related activities (past successes, financial or critical, such as good reviews or shows, even if prior to the relevant five-year period).

• History of the activity's income or losses (such as increases in receipts from year to year unless losses vastly exceed receipts over a long period of time).

• The amount of profits, if any, that are earned.

• Financial status (wealth sufficient to support a hobby would weigh against the profit motive).

• Elements of personal pleasure. (If significant traveling produces few craft objects, the court may be suspicious.)

No single factor will determine the results.

Once you have established yourself as engaged in a craft as a business, all your ordinary and necessary expenditures for production are deductible business expenses. This would include equipment and supplies, work space, office equipment, research or professional books and magazines, travel for business purposes, certain conference fees, agents' commissions, postage, and legal and accounting fees. One of the most significant and problematic of these deductible expenses is the *work space deduction*, discussed in the preceding chapter.

OTHER PROFESSIONAL EXPENSES

Of the ordinary and necessary expenditures involved in the doing of craft, most are classified as *current expenses*: i.e., items with a useful life of less than one year. Raw materials such as clay or fiber, small tools such as pliers and screwdrivers, and postage are all current expenses, fully deductible in the year incurred.

Some business expenses, however, cannot be fully deducted

in the year incurred and must be depreciated. These costs are *capital expenditures*. Professional equipment such as lathes, saws, pottery wheels, looms and the like, with useful lives of more than one year, are capital expenditures that cannot be fully deducted in the year of purchase. Instead, the taxpayer must depreciate, or allocate, the cost of the item over its estimated useful life. This is sometimes referred to as *capitalizing* the cost. Although the actual useful life of equipment will vary, the Code has established fixed periods over which depreciation may be deducted.

The capitalization exemption for free-lance authors, photographers and artists has *not* been interpreted to apply to craftworkers.

In some cases it may be difficult to decide whether an expense is a capital expenditure or a current expense. Equipment repair is one example. If you spend $200 servicing a kiln, this may or may not be a capital expenditure. The general test is whether the amount spent restoring the equipment adds to its value or substantially prolongs its useful life. The cost of replacing short-lived parts to keep equipment in efficient working condition does not substantially add to the useful life of the equipment, so that cost would be a current cost, and fully deductible. The reconditioning of equipment or repairs in the nature of replacement, on the other hand, significantly extend the equipment's useful life; thus, the costs of these are capital expenditures and must be depreciated.

For many craft businesses, an immediate deduction can be taken when equipment is purchased. Up to $10,000 of such purchases may be "expensed" each year, and need not be depreciated. This is called the "election to expense certain depreciable business assets." In order to take advantage of this provision, you must have a net income of at least the amount of the deduction. Excesses can be carried over to the next tax year.

Commissions paid to sales agents, as well as fees to lawyers or accountants, are generally deductible as current expenses, provided they are incurred as a result of a business transaction or paid to preserve existing business goodwill or the like. The same is true of salaries paid to assistants and others whose services are necessary for the business. If you hire help, it is a good idea to hire people on an individual project basis as independent contractors rather than regular employees. This allows you to avoid liability for social security, disability, and withholding tax payments. (You must, however, file a form 1099 MISC for independent contractors who earn $600 or more.) In addition, you should specify to the worker the job-by-job basis of the assignments, state when each project is to be completed, but not the actual hours to be worked and, if possible, allow the person to choose the place to do the work (since this emphasizes the person's independence).

TRAVEL, ENTERTAINMENT AND CONVENTIONS

Craftspeople may travel abroad in order to sell work or gather materials and ideas. More common is the craftworker who might visit another area of the United States.

Although travel solely for educational purposes is not deductible, there may be tax benefits available if trips are business oriented. For a business trip, whether within the U.S. or abroad, ordinary and necessary expenses may be deductible if the travel is solely for business purposes. Transportation costs are fully deductible, except for "luxury water travel," as are costs of lodging away from home on business. However, as of 1987, only 80 percent of the costs of business meals, and meals consumed while on a business trip is deductible, provided these expenses are directly related to the conduct of business.

If the trip is primarily for business, but part of the time is given to a personal vacation; you must indicate which expenses are for business and which for pleasure. This is *not* true in the case of foreign trips if one of the following exceptions applies:
• You had no control over arranging the trip;
• The trip was for a week or less; or
• The nonbusiness activity did not consume 25 percent or more of the total travel time.

If you are claiming one of these exceptions, be careful to have supporting documentation. If you cannot take advantage of one of these exceptions, then you must allocate expenses for the trip abroad according to the percentage of the trip devoted to business versus vacation.

Though the above rules cover business travel both inside and outside of the United States, the rules for deducting expenses incurred for conventions and conferences held outside of the U.S. are more stringent. The IRS tends to review more carefully any deductions for attendance at business seminars that also involve a family vacation, whether inside the U.S. or abroad. In order to deduct the business expense, the taxpayer must be able to document that the reason for attending the meeting was to promote production of income.

Normally, for a spouse's expenses to be deductible, the spouse's presence must be required by the craftworker's employer. In the case of an independent craftsperson who has organized into a partnership or corporation, it is wise to make the spouse a partner, employee, or member of the board. Often seminars will offer special activities for husbands and wives that will provide the needed documentation later on.

As a general rule, the business deductions are for conventions and seminars held in North America. For conventions held outside of North America, deductions are allowed only if the taxpayer establishes that the convention is directly related to the active conduct of his or her trade or business. A number of factors are relevant including the purpose of the meeting, the activities of the sponsoring organizations, and the places where other meetings have been held in the past.

The IRS looks closely at cruise ship seminars and now requires that detailed documentation be attached to the tax return when such seminars are involved. One statement should substantiate the number of days on ship, the number of hours per day spent on business, and the activities in the program. A second statement must come from the sponsor of the convention verifying the first statement. In addition, the ship must be registered in the U.S., or its possessions. Again, the key for the tax-payer taking this sort of deduction is to be sure to provide careful documentation and substantiation.

Whether inside or outside the U.S., the definition of a "business day" can be very helpful in determining whether a trip is deductible. Travel days, including the day of departure and the day of return, count as business days if business activities occurred on such days. If travel is outside the U.S., the same rules apply if the trip is for more than seven days. *Any day the taxpayer uses for business counts as a business day even if only part of the day is spent on business.* A day in which business is canceled through no fault of the taxpayer counts as a business day. Saturdays, Sundays and holidays count as business days even though no business is conducted, provided business is conducted on the Friday before and the Monday after the weekend, or on the days on either side of the holiday.

Entertainment expenses incurred for developing an existing business are deductible in the amount of 80 percent of the actual cost. These expenses must have a proximate relationship to the trade or business and be of the type reasonably expected to benefit the trade or business. You must be especially careful about recording entertainment expenses. You should record in your logbook the amount, date, place, type of entertainment, business purpose, substance of the discussion, participants in the discussion, and the business relationship of the parties you entertained. Keep receipts for any expenses over $25.

You should also keep in mind the stipulation in the tax code which disallows deductions for expenses which are "lavish or extravagant under the circumstances," even though no guidelines have been developed as the definition of "lavish or extravagant." If tickets to a sporting, cultural, or other event are purchased, only the face value of the ticket is deductible. If a skybox or other luxury box seat is purchased or leased and is used for business entertaining, the maximum deduction allowed is the cost of a nonluxury box seat.

A logbook or expense diary is the best line of defense with respect to business expenses incurred while traveling. When on the road, keep the following things in mind:

- With respect to *travel expenses*:

  Keep proof of costs.

  Record the time of departure.

  Record the number of days spent on business.

  List the places visited.

  Note the business purposes of your activities.

- With respect to *transportation costs*:

  Keep copies of all receipts in excess of $25.

  Keep track of all mileage if traveling by car.

  Log all other expenses in your logbook.

Similarly with meals, tips, and lodging, keep receipts for all items over $25. Be sure to record less expensive items in your logbook.

Craftspeople may also take tax deductions for attendance at workshops, seminars, retreats, and the like, provided they carefully document the business nature of the trip. Educational expenses are deductible if the program is meant to maintain or improve current skills, however, the costs of acquiring new skills, or meeting the minimum educational qualifications of your trade or business, are not deductible.

Craftmakers are also able to deduct dues paid to trade associations; however, if a substantial amount of the money goes towards lobbying efforts or other legislative activities of the association, the deductible amount of the dues is limited to that portion which does not support such activities. Any initiation fee or initial expense to join an association is a capital expense and cannot be deducted in the year incurred; it cannot be depreciated since there is no measurable useful life of membership.

CHARITABLE DEDUCTIONS

The law regarding charitable deductions of a craftsperson's own work is not very advantageous. Individuals who donate items they have created may deduct only the cost of materials used to create those works. This provision has had unfortunate effects on libraries and museums, which, since the law's passage in 1969, have experienced enormous decreases in charitable contributions from authors, artists, and craftspeople. The Museum of Modern Art, for example, received fifty-two paintings and sculptures from artists from 1967 to 1969; between 1972 and 1975, only one work was donated.

Art and craft dealers are allowed to deduct the amount paid for the donated object. Collectors can, generally, deduct the fair market value of the piece determined at the time of the donation. There is, however, one exception to the general rule for collectors and that is the "alternative minimum tax" (AMT). Congress has attempted to close loopholes in the tax system while continuing to encourage certain income-producing practices. The AMT, strengthened in 1986, requires that all taxpayers pay a minimum tax percentage even though a taxpayer's income may come from those practices that Congress wishes to encourage. Under this system, the income base is broadened to encompass income from these preferential practices; however, a lower rate is then applied to the income base. Prior law allowed the unrealized appreciation on donated property to be excluded from the income base. The 1986 law adds this unrealized amount back into the income base, thereby giving the collector a deduction of the price paid for the donated piece.

Current tax law puts a further barrier in the way of charitable donations by requiring that a deduction may be taken only by those who itemize. The previous law allowed a charitable deduction whether the taxpayer itemized or simply took the standard deduction.

Although several modifications of the law have been proposed, Congress continues to resist change in the area of tax treatment regarding individuals' donations of their own work. Some states, however, have been more responsive. Oregon and Arkansas now allow creators to deduct the fair market value of their works donated to qualified charities, provided certain criteria are met; and California treats creative property as a capital asset.

GRANTS, PRIZES, AND AWARDS

Craftspeople who receive income from grants or fellowships should be aware that this income can be excluded from gross income and thus may represent considerable tax savings. To qualify for this exclusion, the grant must be for the purpose of furthering the craftsperson's education and training. If the grant is given as compensation for services or is primarily for the benefit of the grant-giving organization, it cannot be excluded. If, however, all degree candidates are required to perform certain services as a condition of receiving the degree, the grant is not considered partial payment for services and is excluded from income. Amounts received under a grant or fellowship that are specifically designated to cover related expenses for the purpose of the grant are no longer fully deductible.

For scholarships and fellowships granted after August 16, 1986, the above deductions are allowed only if the recipient is a degree candidate; and the amount of the exclusion from income is limited to amounts used for tuition, fees, books, supplies and equipment. Amounts designated for room, board, and other incidental expenses are considered income. No exclusions from income are allowed for recipients who are not degree candidates.

The above rules apply to income from grants and fellowships. Unfortunately, the Tax Reform Act of 1986 also put tighter restrictions on money, goods, or services received as prizes or awards. Previously, some awards were excluded from income in certain cases where the recipient was rewarded for past achievements and had not applied for the award. Under the Tax Reform Act of 1986, any prizes or awards for charitable, scientific, or artistic achievements are included in the recipient's income *unless* the prize is assigned to charity, in which case the recipient is not required to render substantial future services as a condition of receiving the award. The recipient must also have been selected without having taken any action to receive the prize.

In conclusion, even though many craftspeople do not consider themselves businesspersons, they may be taxed as such. Because many of the tax provisions designed to encourage the investment end of business are not available to craftspeople, creative people need to concentrate on other methods of reducing taxes. The methods discussed here—income spreading and taking advantage of a variety of deductions—provide a starting point for reducing taxes. Be careful to avoid going beyond the realm of acceptable tax planning. If a particular deduction is questionable, consult with a competent CPA or tax advisor before taking it. In any case, consultation with competent tax professionals is always advisable to ensure maximum benefits.

7

COPYRIGHT

Copyright law in the United States has its foundation in the Constitution, which provides in Article 1, Section 8 that Congress shall have the power "to promote the progress of science and useful arts, by securing for limited time to authors and inventors the exclusive right to their respective writings and discoveries." The first Congress exercised this power and enacted a copyright law. The legislation was periodically revised by later Congresses until 1909. The 1909 Act was substantially revised in 1976, and again in 1988 when the United States became a signatory nation to the Berne Convention, an international copyright treaty.

Prior to the 1976 revision, unpublished works were protected by a so-called common law "copyright" and the various state laws. This was confusing to the individual attempting to secure copyright protection. Federal protection under the 1909 Act was not triggered until publication. Under the 1909 Act, publication meant an unrestricted public display of the work.

The Copyright Revision Act of 1976 preempted the copyright field, making claims after January 1, 1978 subject to federal law only. Publication under this revision is defined as the distribution of copies of a work to the public by some method of ownership transfer such as a sale, or by lease or loan. The creation of copyright in works published prior to January 1, 1978, however, is still governed by the 1909 law.

The Berne Convention Implementation Act of 1988 applies to claims arising after March 1, 1989. One of the major changes in copyright law under the Berne Convention is that, for the first time, United States copyright law does not require a copyright notice, although notice is recommended when possible.

In effect, there are three sets of laws in the field of copyright. The craftmaker must be aware of the differences in order to fully benefit from the law.

WHAT IS COPYRIGHT?

There are five exclusive rights included in the "bundle of rights" known as copyright. The first is the right of first publication, which is the right to determine when and where your work will first be displayed to the general public or a substantial number of persons outside of family members and social acquaintances. If you have sold a copyrighted work, however, the buyer now has the right to display that work as he or she sees fit. The buyer, however, does not have the right to reproduce the work.

Second is the right to control the first sale of a work. The only exception may be in cases where lienholders who were involved in producing or processing the work levy upon it for the satisfaction of unpaid debts. There is a difference between conveying the copyright in a work, which can only be done through a signed writing, and selling the actual piece. Once a work is sold, the control over that piece ends, unless there is a contract restricting the purchaser's use.

Third is the right to reproduce the work once it has been copyrighted. The Copyright Act of 1976 allows reproduction of works in a few limited circumstances, and applies the concept of the *fair use doctrine*, which will be explained later in this chapter.

Fourth is the right to prepare derivative works based on the copyrighted work. A derivative work is some form of adaptation or transformation of the original work.

Fifth is the right to publicly perform the copyrighted work (where applicable).

These rights are divisible, meaning that they can be transferred in whole or in part. If you take no special action when you sell a work, you will retain all of the above rights. You may, however, explicitly transfer or license a particular right if you wish. In order to do so, the transfer must be in writing, signed by the copyright owner or an authorized agent, and must identify the right(s) to be conveyed. A license can be oral, however, it is revocable at the will of the copyright owner.

The copyright law itself does not provide economic benefits. The law vests intangible rights in the copyright owner which allows the owner to bargain for future economic benefits such as royalties on reproductions.

WHAT CAN BE COPYRIGHTED?

Copyright protection extends to "works of original authorship fixed in any tangible medium of expression." It does not, however, extend to any "idea, procedure, process, system, method of operation, concept, principle or discovery." Copyright is protection for the form of expression and not the idea expressed. Therefore, an idea for a piece of jewelry cannot be copyrighted but the tangible expression of that idea, a ring for example, is eligible for copyright protection. An author, from the copyright standpoint, may be the creator—be it potter, jeweler, writer or photographer, or the employer in a work-for-hire situation.

The 1909 Act required the work to be both original and creative in order to obtain copyright protection. The creativity prerequisite was expressly dropped from the law in 1976, although there is a presumption that minimal creativity must exist in the creation of the work. The requirement that a work be original does not mean that the work must be unique. Originality means that the work was not copied from another.

Example: Suppose you create a silver bracelet in a limited edition of twenty. The design on each bracelet is copyrightable because it is original although it is not unique. If, by some miracle of circumstances, another silversmith independently creates a bracelet identical to any of the ones you have created, his or her bracelet is eligible for copyright protection as well because it satisfies the originality requirement. If, however, the other artist copied your work, he or she would be an infringer. The infringing work would be denied copyright protection, and the infringer would likely be liable to you for damages.

Cartographers who independently create identical maps of a geographic area are each entitled to copyright protection because each is original in its creation. Many cartographers will intentionally include a minor error on a map so that if the identical error appears on another map alleged to be original, there will be obvious evidence that copying has occurred. Thus, in the writing of this book, I have intentionally included minor (?) errors to inhibit copyright infringement.

WHO OWNS THE COPYRIGHT?

Generally, the creator of the copyrighted work is the owner of the copyright. There are, however, exceptions to this general rule. The 1909 law provided that copyright ownership passed from the creator to the purchaser of the work unless the creator explicitly retained ownership. As such, when a potter sold a copyrighted pot, the purchaser received not only the pot, but the copyright in the pot as well. The presumption was that copyright went with the sale of the work.

In 1968, New York recognized the unfairness of this policy and passed legislation reversing this presumption. California followed suit shortly thereafter. These state laws applied only to those works sold in the states between the time the legislation was enacted and the effective date of the 1976 Act.

The Copyright Revision Act of 1976 adopts the New York and California provisions and reverses the presumption that the copyright goes with the sale of the work. Today, there must be a written agreement providing for the sale of the copyright, otherwise the creator of the work remains the copyright owner. Ownership of the work is recognized as distinct from ownership of the copyright. If the potter wishes to transfer the copyright along with the ownership of the pot, itself, he or she may do so through a written document.

JOINT WORKS

In a joint work, each contributor automatically acquires an individual ownership in the entire work. Section 201(a) of the Copyright Act provides, "The authors of a joint work are co-owners of copyright in the work." A *joint work* is defined as "a work prepared by two or more authors with the intention that their contributions be merged into inseparable or interdependent parts of a unitary whole." Thus, whatever profit one co-owner makes from a joint work must be shared equally with the other co-owners, unless they have a written agreement stating otherwise.

The key point is the intent that the parts be absorbed or combined into an integrated unit at the time the work is created. The late Professor Melville Nimmer suggested that although such an intent must exist at the time the work is created, not at a later date, the authors do not necessarily have to work together, work during the same period, or even know each other. However, the joint works definition does not include the situation where an artist creates a work, such as a piano solo, not intending that the work involve another artist, and later commissions lyrics.

If there is no intention to create a unitary or indivisible work, each creator owns the copyright only to his or her individual contribution. In *Ashton-Tate Corp. v. Ross*, the Ninth Circuit Court of Appeals held that joint authorship was not established by the mere contribution of ideas and guidance for the user interface of a computer spreadsheet, because the joint authorship requires each author to make an independently copyrightable contribution.

DERIVATIVE WORKS

In the case of a *derivative work*, the contributing author owns only his own contribution. A derivative work is defined as:

A work based upon one or more preexisting works, such as a translation, fictionalization, motion picture version, sound recording, art reproduction, abridgement, condensation, or any other form in which a work may be recast, transformed, or adapted. A work consisting of editorial revisions, annotations, elaborations, or other modifications which, as a whole, represent an original work of authorship, is a "derivative work." (17 U.S.C. § 101)

Thus, any work based completely or substantially upon a preexisting work, if it satisfies the originality requirement, and is not itself an infringing work, will be separately copyrightable. The distinction between a derivative work and a joint work lies in the intent of each contributor at the time the contribution is created. If the work is created with the intention that each contribution be merged into inseparable or interdependent parts of a "unitary whole," then the merger creates a joint work. If such intention occurs only after the work has been created, then the merger results in a derivative or collective work.

COLLECTIVE WORKS

A *collective work* is defined as "a work, such as a periodical issue, anthology, or encyclopedia, in which a number of contributions, constituting separate and independent works in themselves, are assembled into a collective whole." (17 U.S.C. § 101)

The originality involved in a collective work is the collection and assembling of preexisting works, which are themselves capable of copyright, without any internal changes in such material. This assemblage of work is copyrightable.

WORKS FOR HIRE

There is an important exception to the copyright ownership rule in the form of the *works-for-hire* doctrine. Employers, under this classification, are granted the copyright in works created by their employees if that creation is within the scope of the employee's job. The rationale for this exception is that the employee has already been rewarded for creating the copyrightable material by a salary from the employer. The employer's investment must now be protected from competitors by making use of the property created by the employee. The work-for-hire doctrine arose from this set of circumstances and is based on several grounds: (1) the work is produced on behalf of the employer and under his or her direction; (2) the employee is paid for the work; and (3) the employer, having paid all the costs and bearing all the risks of loss, should reap any gain.

A work for hire is defined as a "work made by an employee within the scope of his or her employment." Therefore, if a silversmith is an employee and creates a piece of jewelry within his or her scope of employment, the copyright belongs to the employer.

The work-for-hire provisions of the 1909 Act have been shown in studies by the Copyright Office to have been a historical misstep in terms of the legislative process. The focus of Congress was on staff-written material prepared by salaried employees for publication by an employer-publisher in composite or encyclopedic works. The copyright studies suggest that the legislators did not realize the breadth of the exception they were creating since it could be applied to a variety of employment situations such as full-time crafts teachers.

THE UNDEFINABLE AUTHOR

There has been much discussion about the definition of the word *author* in the statute. One early draft of the 1909 bill defined author as including "an employer, in the case of a work produced by an employee during the hours for which his salary is paid, subject to any agreement to the contrary." This provision was added at the request of publishers of encyclopedias, directories, and other written composite works, and the publishers of prints and similar graphic arts. The purpose was to make sure that they could secure copyright in the materials written by their staffs. The definition was criticized as being too elaborate.

Other proposals were made, which were also criticized. The language of other bills, "and the word author shall include an employer in the case of works made for hire," contained no definition at all. Nevertheless, this language was enacted without change or discussion, and remained until the 1976 revision. The 1976 Act provides that under certain circumstances the employer *is* the author and owns the copyright in works made for hire.

IMPRACTICALITY OF SHARED COPYRIGHT

There were some proposals, during the hearings on the 1976 Act, to let the employer acquire the right to an employee's work to the extent needed for regular business purposes, but allowing the employee to own all other rights as long as the employee did not authorize competing uses. These proposals were not adopted for several reasons: the difficulty of defining what uses of a work were competing, the impracticality of applying the language to situations where the work was a composite of many employees, and a potential user's inability to identify owners for the purpose of negotiations.

Although there are no concrete definitions of *employee* or *scope of employment*, the courts have established guidelines for determining whether a work is one made for hire. One element is the existence of an express contract for hire, especially if the author agrees to work exclusively for the employer. Payment of a regular salary is also an important factor. Some courts have found that the crucial question in determining an employment relationship is whether the alleged employer has the right to direct and supervise the manner in which the other person performs the work.

Even if there is a clear employer-employee relationship, the mere fact that an employee creates a work is not enough to make that work a work for hire. It is only when an employee creates a work within the scope of his or her employment that the creation is a work made for hire. As one court said in regard to no less a person than Admiral Hyman Rickover, "No one sells or mortgages all the products of his brain to his employer by the mere fact of employment." (*Public Affairs Associates, Inc. v. Rickover* [1959].) Thus, the artistic efforts of an employee not produced within the scope of employment remain the property of the employee.

SPECIAL EMPLOYEE DOCTRINE

Under previous law a person, although seemingly an independent craftmaker, was considered an employee if he or she was subject to the supervision or control of the person commissioning the work. The craftmaker was considered a *special employee* in this case and the copyright belonged to the person who commissioned the work.

Community for Creative Non-Violence (CCNV) v. Reid overruled this doctrine. Reid, the sculptor, agreed with CCNV to sculpt three figures huddled over a steam grate for a nativity scene depicting the plight of the homeless. CCNV would provide the pedestal and steam grate for the scene. The parties negotiated the price and the materials to be used and CCNV made recommendations concerning the figures themselves. Copyright ownership was not discussed. A dispute arose after the project had been completed and each party filed for copyright registration. Although the lower court determined that the project fell under the work-for-hire doctrine and CCNV owned the copyright, the appellate court reversed. The sculpture did not fall under one of the enumerated classes of projects outlined in the law as being potentially a work-for-hire and there was no writing as required by the law.

The copyright statute now recognizes a long-standing trade practice that the copyright of certain works created by independent contractors or by employees outside the scope of their employment belongs to the creator rather than the employer, unless the parties expressly agree in writing that the piece shall be considered a work for hire. Thus, a work specially ordered or commissioned is *not* presumed to be a work-for-hire *unless* it is intended as:

• a contribution to a collective work;
• part of a movie or other audiovisual work;
• a translation, supplement, or compilation;
• an instructional text;
• a test or answer material for a test; or
• an atlas.

THE WORKS-FOR HIRE DOCTRINE AND THE CRAFTWORKER/TEACHER

Many artists and craftspeople who are employed in educational institutions remain active and prolific in their creative fields. For some, creating works of art or craft is a way to further explore the subject they teach, a way to remain creative; for others it may be a way of supplementing their salaries. It is important to determine whether the artist or craftsperson owns the rights to designs they create, or whether the employer owns the rights. In this section, discussion will focus on whether works created by a craftsperson or artist who is employed at an educational institution are *works for hire*, and whether the institution owns the copyright.

It is important to determine whether these works are made for hire, not only because of the implications of copyright ownership, but also because ownership affects copyright renewal. Under the 1909 law, the holder of a copyright is the only person eligible to renew the copyright. Under current copyright law, the term of copyright for works for hire is one hundred years from the creation or seventy-five years from first publication, whichever expires first. In many cases this will be shorter than the usual term of "life of the author plus fifty years." Also, works for hire are not subject to the termination provisions of the statute, which allow an artist, craftmaker or others to terminate the assignment of a grant or transfer of rights.

One of the key elements in a work-for-hire situation is whether the employer has the right to supervise or control the person performing the work. In academic settings professors write and deliver lectures virtually without administrative control. However, there is some control since the courses that the professor is hired to teach determine, within certain bounds, what the subject matter of the lectures should be. Also, the quality of teaching is reviewed by the administration. Since there are elements of control, and teachers or professors receive regular compensation and have express contracts for hire, two other factors that the courts consider, they probably are engaged in employment for hire.

It is important to determine the *scope* of the employment situation. A great source of litigation in the scope-of-employment area is the employee's creation of a work relating to the job but which is not a part of his or her specific duties. This is the case, for example, when a teacher creates a work of art or craft in the teacher's particular field, but the work was not expressly mentioned as one of the teacher's duties.

In determining scope of employment, control and supervision are crucial issues. Factors to consider are whether the work was edited by the employer, or whether there was any control over content and style of the work. Artists and craftspeople can argue that their school/employer has no such control or supervision.

A second criterion to be considered is whether the work was created at the employer's place of business. It generally cannot be assumed that a teacher will or will not use the facilities of the school to create independent projects. However, it has been held that if a work would not otherwise fall within the scope of employment, the fact that a portion of the work was done using the employer's facilities and personnel does not necessarily render the work the property of the employer.

A third issue is whether the work was created during normal working hours. This may be an unimportant distinction in regard to teachers or professors since the concept of nine-to-five working hours often is not applicable. Schools usually do not dictate class preparation time, and it is sometimes difficult to distinguish between a professor's working hours and leisure time. This criterion might more readily apply to elementary or high school teachers who in general have more regular hours. However, even they are more flexible in the time they work than a factory worker, for example.

The final criterion for determining whether a work was created within the scope of employment is whether it was produced at the insistence and expense of the employer, i.e., was the employer the motivating factor in producing the work? The outcome of this test depends on the facts of each case. A weaving instructor who creates a rug while demonstrating to the class an intricate weaving pattern is more likely to have created a work for hire than if she had created a rug on her own time, using her own loom.

There are some situations in the realm of education in which good arguments can be made that the work was not created within the scope of employment. However, if the educational institution has any control over the work, or the work is done at the time, place, expense, or insistence of the institution, it is probably a work made for hire, and the institution would own the copyright.

Creative people in the education sector should take some steps to avoid the injustice of the work-for-hire doctrine because many works created by artists or craftspeople who are also employed by educational institutions might be considered works made for hire.

One possible step would be for you to obtain a transfer of copyright ownership from the school. To be valid, there must be a note or memorandum of the transfer, signed by an agent of the school.

A second option is to vary ownership rights through a written contract between the parties involved. The Copyright Act provides: "In the case of a work made for hire, the employer or other person for whom the work was prepared is considered the author for purposes of this title, and unless the parties have expressly agreed otherwise in a written instrument signed by them, owns all the rights comprised in the copyright." Thus, a teacher and the school could include a provision in their contract to negate the presumption that the school owns the copyright. This provision must be definite and precisely state what the rights are that the employee retains.

While the parties may vary the rights that would otherwise be owned by the employer, they cannot vary the employer's status as author of the work. This distinction in the Act was intentional, and was made in order to prevent parties from avoiding the legal consequences (other than ownership rights) that arise by reason of the status of a work as one made for hire.

Finally, the present copyright law could be revised to define such creations by teachers as being outside the scope of their employment. One case, *Williams v. Weisser*, 78 Cal. Rptr. 542 (1962), held that a U.C.L.A. professor, rather than the university that employed him, owned the common law copyright to his lectures. The court recognized the custom that faculty members retain the common law right to their lectures. Although the 1976 Act preempts common law copyright, such reasoning could still be used to persuade Congress to change the existing law.

DURATION OF COPYRIGHT

The Constitution allows Congress to extend copyright protection for "limited times." The 1909 Act granted protection for twenty-eight years, with an additional renewal period of twenty-eight years. In 1976, the revision Act generally extended the copyright protection to the life of the creator plus fifty years.

For works created on or after the effective date of the Act, January 1, 1978, the protection period is the life of the author plus fifty years. In work-for-hire situations or when the author is anonymous or uses a pseudonym, the period of protection is 100 years from creation or 75 years from publication whichever expires first. The same periods of protection are given those works created before January 1, 1978, but not published (or registered) prior to that date. These works do not fit under the 1909 provisions because the 1909 Act protects only published works. Because these works were in tangible form prior to the 1976 Act, they do not automatically fall within the protection of that Act either. The earliest date a copyright can expire under this provision is December 31, 2002. If the work is published by that date, there is an extension of twenty-five years from the date the copyright would have expired under the old law.

No renewals are obtainable under the 1976 Act, except for those works granted copyright protection under the 1909 Act. If a copyrighted work was not yet into the final renewal period under the 1909 Act, an additional renewal period of forty-seven years is granted after the first term expires. For works that were in the renewal period at the time the 1976 Act took effect, there is an automatic extension of the number of years that would create a seventy-five year total from the copyright date.

CREATION

Federal copyright law now protects works once they are fixed in tangible form. There are no longer formal requirements of registration, however, in order to bring an infringement suit, there must be a copyright registration. You can register after the infringement has occurred provided it is before the lawsuit is filed. If you register early, there is the added advantage that the information in the registration is presumed to be true after five years. This is so even if you register prior to publication but publish before the five-year period expires.

NOTICE

Under the 1909 Act, notice was required on published works. If notice did not appear on the work it was considered, with few exceptions, to be in the public domain. Notice had to appear on the original and all copies. If affixing notice on certain works would impair the value of the work, less conspicuous notice requirements were available. Publication triggered copyright protection under the 1909 law.

For example, the city of Chicago, in *Letters Edged in Black Press, Inc. v. Chicago*, lost the copyright on Picasso's sculpture "The Chicago Picasso" because a maquette of the work was placed on public exhibition at the Art Institute without a copyright notice attached. Photographs of the maquette, also without notice, were distributed to the press. The court ruled that the exhibition of the maquette without notice, as well as the distribution of the photographs, caused the work to fall into the public domain. The notice attached to the completed sculpture was invalid because this sculpture was, in the court's words, "a mere copy, albeit on a grand scale, of the maquette, a work already in public domain."

The 1976 Revision Act provides protection once the work is in tangible form, whether it has been published or not. However, prior to March 1989, in order to retain copyright protection after publication, notice must have appeared on the work. If the notice was omitted from a small number of copies, the work is registered within five years of publication and a reasonable effort is made to affix notice on all works distributed in the United States, or notice was omitted by a third party in violation of an express agreement only to distribute copies with proper notice, the copyright is not lost.

The 1976 revision would likely change the result in a situation similar to "The Chicago Picasso" case. Any one of the three provisions could be used to save the copyright under the right circumstances.

The 1988 Implementation Act eliminates the requirement for

notice on any works that are published after March 1, 1989. But, notice is still required for works published prior to March 1, 1989. There are, however, advantages to continuing to affix notice to works even though it is not required by law. One advantage is that in a copyright infringement suit, the defense of "innocent infringement" is not available if there is proper notice on the work. Innocent infringement involves someone copying a work believing that it is in the public domain. Notice attached to the work eliminates this argument. Also, attaching notice to works is an inexpensive way to deter potential infringers. It is therefore wise to continue to attach notice to copyrighted works in order to prevent any claim of innocent infringement.

Proper notice consists of three elements. The first is the word *copyright*, the abbreviation *Copr.*, or the letter *c* in a circle, ©. Second is the year of first publication, or registration if the governing law is the 1909 Act. There is a narrow list of exceptions for this requirement under the 1976 Act. The name of the copyright owner is the third element of notice. The name should be the author's full name unless the author is well known by last name only.

International notice requirements differ somewhat from the requirements imposed by the 1976 Act. For countries that are covered by the Buenos Aires Convention, another copyright treaty to which the United States is a party, the words *all rights reserved* must appear in either English or Spanish. If you plan on selling your works in Central or South America, be sure to investigate any special international notice requirements that may be in effect. The Berne Convention prohibits signatory nations from requiring that notice be placed on works in order to obtain protection. There are more than 80 countries which participate in this treaty. The Universal Copyright Convention, the third copyright treaty to which the United States is a party, requires the use of the symbol © as part of the copyright notice for protection under it. Most Western European countries as well as the Soviet Union are parties to this treaty.

FILING AN APPLICATION AND DEPOSITING THE WORK

Registration with the Copyright Office and filing an application for a copyright are not prerequisites for creating a federal copyright under the law. The Copyright Revision Act of 1976 requires registration only (1) as a prerequisite to commencing an infringement action, (2) when the copyright owner wishes to take advantage of the savings provision discussed in the notice Section of this Chapter or (3) if the Register of Copyrights demands registration of published works bearing a copyright notice. The Berne Convention does not eliminate registration but provides that registration is not required from copyright proprietors in other Berne signatory nations.

The law separates registration from deposit requirements. Under the 1909 Act, registration involved filing a copyright application, paying a $6 fee and depositing two copies of the work itself, or two photographs of the original with the Copyright Office in Washington, D.C. However, "fine prints" came within the requirements of actual copies and thus it was necessary to deposit two actual prints.

The law now recognizes the economic hardship this caused artists and the fact that many artists intentionally failed to take advantage of copyright protection because of the burdensome deposit requirements. The Register of Copyrights is allowed to exempt certain categories from the deposit requirements or provide for alternative forms of deposit. Fine prints in editions less than 300 are exempt from the requirement of providing actual copies; photographs will suffice.

A craftmaker should deposit two of the "best" copies of the work to be copyrighted with the Library of Congress, Washington, D.C. 20559, within three months of publication (creation). If the objects are bulky, fragile, or valuable, photographs may be deposited instead of the actual work. The application and the filing fee, which is now $20, need not be submitted with the copies. The Register of Copyrights can demand these copies even if there is no registration. Failure to respond to this demand can result in a $250 fine for each unsubmitted work.

Although you can delay registration, there are at least two reasons why a craftmaker should deposit the work and register the copyright within three months of publication. The first is that the copyright law prohibits the awarding of attorney fees and statutory damages for infringements that occur prior to registration. This means that you are limited to actual damages. The second reason is that if you deposit the required two copies within the three-month period but fail to register, the Copyright Office will require two more copies of the work when you eventually do send in the registration form and filing fee.

The copyright in the work is registered once you receive back the form you submitted with the Copyright Office's registration number. Store this document in a safe place; it is your official record of registration and you will need to produce it in the event of litigation for infringement.

Copyright laws are extremely beneficial for craftmakers who can take advantage of them. Since the protection is simple to obtain and the cost of copyright registration is relatively low, craftmakers should devote some attention to this means of protection. Readers who desire more information should contact the Copyright Office, Library of Congress, Washington, D.C. 20559, and ask for a free copyright information packet. The registration form you will need is form VA.

INFRINGEMENT

Copyright infringement is the unauthorized use of any of the exclusive rights protected through copyright. The intent of the infringer is relevant only to the question of damages. The federal courts have exclusive jurisdiction over copyright infringement. Actions must be brought within three years of the infringement. The trial judge has wide discretion in setting damages. Under the 1976 Act, as amended, the judge can award actual or statutory damages. The statutory damages range from as little as

$200 for an innocent infringement to between $500 and $20,000 for the unintentional case, and up to $100,000 if the infringement is willful. Criminal prosecution is also available, theoretically; however, it is quite uncommon. If found guilty, the infringer faces a $10,000 fine and up to one year in prison.

In order to prove infringement, the copyright owner must prove that the work was copyrighted and registered, the infringer had access to the work and used it in the creation of the infringing work, and that the infringer copied a "substantial and material" portion of the protected work. Even before trial, the copyright owner can obtain an order that allows the court to seize the alleged infringing work. After the trial, if an infringement is found, the infringing work may be destroyed and an injunction issued against future infringement.

FAIR USE

In cases where someone is accused of copyright infringement, a major defense is "fair use," a doctrine that was created and refined by the courts under the 1909 Act. The 1976 Act attempted to codify this judicial development and sets out four factors to guide courts in future applications of the fair use doctrine. They are:

- The purpose and character of the use, including whether such use is of a commercial nature or is for nonprofit educational purposes;
- The nature of the copyrighted work;
- The amount and substantiality of the portion used in relation to the copyrighted work as a whole; and
- The effect of the use upon the potential market for or value of the copyrighted work. (17 U.S.C. § 107)

The United States Supreme Court addressed the fair use doctrine in the realm of motion pictures in *Sony Corporation of America v. Universal Studies, Inc*. The plaintiff movie producers, in this case, claimed that the defendant, Sony, was enabling consumers to violate the copyright law by selling home videotape recorders. Consumers could record copyrighted works off the air. The plaintiffs alleged that Sony should be liable for copyright infringement as a conspirator. The Court concluded that home video recording for noncommercial uses is a fair use of copyrighted material. The majority of the Justices expressly refrained from considering the fair use doctrine in connection with other copyrighted works. Neither Congress nor the courts have yet addressed the likely concerns of artists and craft-workers in the area of fair use.

8

INSURANCE

Today's insurance business originated in a London coffeehouse called Lloyd's sometime in the late seventeenth century. Lloyd's was a popular gathering place for seamen and merchants engaged in foreign trade. As Shakespeare pointed out in *The Merchant of Venice*, great profit can come from a successful sea voyage, but financial disaster can follow just as surely from a loss of ships at sea. From past experience, these merchants knew that despite their greatest precautions, such disaster could strike any one of them.

Through their dealings in Italy, the merchants had become familiar with the notion of insurance, but there was no organized insurance company in England at that time. So, when these merchants were together at Lloyd's, it became a custom to arrange for mutual insurance contracts. The method employed was for a ship's owner, before the ship embarked, to pass around a slip of paper that described the ship, its captain and crew, its destination, and the nature of the cargo. Those merchants who wished to be insurers of that particular ship would initial this slip and indicate the extent to which they could be held liable. This slip was circulated until the entire value of the ship and cargo was covered. This method of creating insurance contracts was called "underwriting."

Today, the term *underwriting* is used to describe the formation of any insurance contract regardless of the means employed in establishing it. Lloyd's of London still uses a method similar to that which originated in the coffeehouse, but most other insurance companies secure against loss out of their own financial holdings.

The risks covered by insurance have changed also. The original Lloyd's dealt in maritime insurance only. Now almost anything can be insured—from a pianist's hands to the Concorde jet.

WHY INSURANCE FOR THE CRAFTSPERSON

Although the business of a craftsperson may not be as perilous as was that of the seventeenth-century merchant seaman, it is not without risks. Some of the more significant risks include:

- Recent crime statistics show that, even in rural areas, the craftsperson may be subject to burglary. Various methods may be employed to protect against burglary, but none is perfect.
- The forces of nature—flood, earthquake, some types of fire— are undiscriminating in their choice of victims. You may already have homeowner's insurance against these, but you may find that your policy is inadequate to cover your works and materials. Your homeowner's insurance may, in fact, not cover these at all, as will be discussed later in this chapter.
- A sale of your work imposes upon you virtually unlimited liability in regard to anyone who may be injured by one of your objects, regardless of how careful you may have been in creating it. The potential magnitude of what this could cost you easily makes even the slightest chance of its occurrence a significant risk. (See Chapter 9, Product Liability.)
- Loss of earnings due to illness or accident is a risk common to all craftmakers. Some craftspeople who rely on one or more partners may suffer a loss of earnings because of a loss of part-

ners through sickness or accident. This risk is far too often overlooked.

All these risks can be insured against through any number of insurance companies. It should be noted, however, that there are some things that you *cannot* insure against. Insurance is similar to gambling in that it involves an outlay of some money and if a certain event occurs, you get back many times more. If it does not occur, you get back nothing. But that is where the similarity ends.

Public policy will not permit you to insure something unless you have an *insurable interest*. To have an insurable interest, you must have a property right, a contract right, or a potential liability that creates a real expectation of loss to you if a given event occurs. The rationale behind this is simply to minimize the temptation to cause the calamity against which you are insured. History contains many gruesome stories of desperate or insane people obtaining insurance on a neighbor's barn or even on a neighbor's child.

Of course, the requirement of an insurable interest has never stopped anyone from hastening that interest's demise or destruction. Recently, two businessmen were overheard at a party. One told the other that he had recovered one million dollars in fire insurance that year. The other businessman said he recovered *two million* for losses caused by a windstorm. The first, with greed in his eyes, asked, "How do you start a windstorm?"

THE BASICS OF INSURANCE LAW

Before analyzing the mechanics of choosing whether to insure a particular risk, a brief outline of the law of insurance may be helpful. All insurance is based on a contract between the insurer and the insured whereby the insurer assumes a specified risk for a fee (the premium). The insurance contract must contain at least the following: (1) a definition of whatever is to be insured (the subject matter); (2) the nature of the risks insured against; (3) the maximum possible recovery; (4) the duration of the insurance; and (5) the due date and amount of premiums. When the amount of recovery has been predetermined in the insurance contract, it is called a *valued* policy. An *unvalued* or *open* insurance policy covers the full current loss of property up to a specified policy limit. The advantages and disadvantages of each will be discussed in this chapter.

The insurance contract does more than merely shift the risk from the insured to the insurance company. The insurance industry is regulated by state law so as to spread the risk among those subject to that same risk. The risk spreading is accomplished by defining the method used for determining the amount of the premium to be paid by the insured. First, the insurance company obtains data on the actual loss sustained by a defined class within a given period of time. State law regulates just how the company may define the class. An insurance company may not, for example, separate white homeowners and non-white homeowners into different classes, but it may separate drivers with many accidents from drivers with few.

The company then divides the risk equally among the members of the class, adds a fee for administrative costs and profits. This amount is regulated from state to state. Finally, the premium is set for each individual in proportion to the likelihood that a loss will occur to him or to her. Besides the method of determining premiums, state insurance laws usually specify the training necessary for agents and brokers, the amount of commission payable to them, and the kind of investments the insurance company may make with the premiums.

The very documents that a company uses to make insurance contracts are likewise state-regulated. States require a standard form from which the company may not deviate, especially for fire insurance. A growing number of states are stipulating that plain English must be used in all forms. "Plain English" is an indexed measure of readability in reference to the average number of syllables per word and the average number of words per sentence. Because of the ruling that insurance contracts are per se fraudulent if they exceed certain maximum averages, the insurance companies have been forced to write contracts that an average consumer can understand.

EXPECTATIONS VERSUS REALITY

One frequent result of the gobbledygook that most insurance contracts are written in is that the signed contract may differ in some respect from what the agent may have led the insured person to expect. If, however, you can prove that an agent actually lied, then the agent will be personally liable to you for the amount of promised coverage.

Most often the agent will not lie but will "accidentally" neglect to inform the insured of some detail. For instance, if you want insurance for transporting your craftwork, the agent may sell you a policy that only covers transport in public carriers when you intended to rent a truck and transport it yourself. In most states, the courts hold that it is the duty of the insured to read the policy before signing it. If, in the above example, you had neglected to read the clause that limits coverage to a public carrier, you would be out of luck. Failure to read the policy is no excuse and do not be bashful about asking questions.

In other, more progressive states, this doctrine has been considered too harsh. Instead, those states will allow an insured to challenge specific provisions in the signed contract to the extent they do not conform to reasonable expectations based upon promises that the agent made. In the example above, it might be considered reasonable to expect that you would be insured when transporting your own goods. If the agent had not specifically brought this limitation in the contract to your attention, odds are that you would have a good case for getting it amended or removed.

Of course, you should not expect an agent to point out these unexpected variations even in the most liberal state. You should read the contract with the agent. If it is unintelligible, ask the agent to list on a separate sheet in plain English all the important aspects before you sign.

REFORMING THE CONTRACT

After the insurance contract has been signed, its terms can be reformed only to comply with the actual original agreement from which the written contract may somehow have deviated. *Example*: in a case where a woman inherited a pearl necklace, an appraiser, apparently hoping for a large fee, misled her and told her the pearls were genuine and therefore worth $60,000. Before having them shipped from the estate, she obtained insurance on them in the amount of $60,000, and paid a premium of $2,450. In the description of the subject matter it was stated that the pearls were genuine. The pearls were ruined after they arrived at the delivery terminal but before she received them. She tried to collect the $60,000.

In the course of the investigation of the accident, it was discovered that the pearls were not genuine but cultured, and were worth only $61.50. Of course, the insured could not collect $60,000 because no genuine pearls had been lost or damaged. The worst of it was that she could not collect even $61.50 because the policy did not cover cultured pearls. The court emphasized that for reformation of the contract to be granted, there must have been something either included or omitted contrary to the intention of both parties. In this case neither party ever intended to include cultured pearls so the court refused to make a contract for the parties covering cultured pearls.

You might think that in this case the insured would get back her premium because there were never any genuine pearls to insure. She argued this but lost again. The court reasoned that had the pearls been lost in transit instead of being later destroyed, the actual value of the pearls would never have come to light. Therefore, the insurance company had indeed assumed the risk of paying out $60,000 and thus was entitled to the premium.

OVERINSURING AND UNDERINSURING

This case does not mean that if an insured accidentally overvalues the goods no insurance will be recovered. Had the pearls been genuine but worth only $20,000 she would have recovered $20,000. Note that overinsurance does not entitle one to a recovery beyond the actual value of the goods insured. This is because one does not have an insurable interest beyond the actual value of an item. Allowing a recovery greater than the value of the goods would be inviting people to gamble with insurance policies.

Since you can, at best, break even with insurance, you might think it would be profitable to underinsure your goods. You could gain by paying lower premiums and lose only in the event that the damage exceeds the policy maximum. This also has been tried and failed.

Let us study a case where the insured stated the value of her unscheduled property as $9,950 and obtained insurance on that amount. *Unscheduled property* means that an unvalued insurance policy is obtained on some undetermined collection of goods—for example, all a person's clothes and furniture, which may change from time to time. In this case, a fire occurred causing at least $9,950 damage.

The insurance company investigated the claim and determined that the insured owned at least $36,500 in unscheduled property. The company refused to pay on grounds that the insured obtained the insurance fraudulently. The court agreed with the insurance company, stating that the intentional failure to communicate the full value of the unscheduled property rendered the entire contract void. The insured, therefore, could not even collect the policy maximum. At best, all she could hope for would be to get her premiums back.

Although at first glance this decision may seem harsh, its ultimate fairness becomes apparent with a little analysis. The chance of losing $9,950 out of $36,500 is greater than the chance of losing $9,950 out of $9,950 simply because most accidents or thefts do not result in total losses. In this case the insured did not pay premiums for $9,950 coverage because she belonged in a much higher risk category.

Various tests are used by the courts to determine whether an omission or misstatement renders a contract void. In all cases the omission or misstatement must be intentional or obviously reckless, and it must be material to the contract. Materiality is measured with reference to the degree of importance that the insurance company assigns to the omitted or misstated fact. If stating the fact correctly would have significantly affected the conditions or premiums that the company would demand, then the fact is material. In the above case, had the full value of the unscheduled property been stated, the insurer would either have demanded that the full value be insured or that a higher premium be paid for the limited coverage. Thus, the misstatement was clearly material.

UNINTENTIONAL UNDERVALUING

It should be noted that not all undervaluations will be considered material. Many insurance contracts do allow some undervaluation where it is unintentional. This provision is designed to protect the insured from inflation, which causes property to increase in replacement value before the policy's renewal date.

A so-called *co-insurance clause* generally provides that the insured may recover 100 percent of any loss up to the face value of the policy provided the property is insured for at least 80 percent of its full value. *Example*: if a house worth $100,000 were insured for $80,000 and suffered a $79,000 loss from a covered casualty, the insured would recover the full amount of the loss, or $79,000. If the same property were only insured for $50,000, then a formula would be used to determine the amount of recovery. This formula is: divide the amount of insurance coverage by the total value of the property, and multiply the resulting fraction by the loss to determine the recovery.

Inserting numbers in the above formula, we have: $50,000

(insurance) ÷by $100,000 (value of building) × $79,000 (loss) = $39,500 (recovery). This example points out the importance of carrying insurance on at least 80 percent of the value of your property. In view of recent inflation rates, it would be wise to re-examine your coverage each year.

All insurance policies are limited to certain defined subject matter and to losses caused to that subject matter by certain defined risks. Once the risks are recognized, it is a simple matter to decide whether or not to insure against them. Correctly defining the subject matter of insurance is, however, tricky business. Mistakes here are not uncommon and can result in any one of us finding ourselves uninsured—like the woman with the pearl necklace.

SCHEDULING PROPERTY

The typical insurance policy will include various exclusions and exemptions. For example, most homeowner and auto insurance policies cover personal property but exclude business property. If a craftsperson keeps certain works at home for personal enjoyment, are they personal or business property? The answer depends on whether the craftmaker ever sells or publicly displays any of these works. If any are sold or publicly displayed, this may convert the entire holding to business property.

In order to avoid the potentially tragic loss of such property, the craftsperson may schedule the pieces that are held for personal enjoyment. *Scheduling* is a form of inventorying where the insured submits a list and description of all pieces to be insured with an appraisal of their value. The insurer assumes the risk of loss of all scheduled works without concern as to whether they pertain to business or not. Insurance on scheduled property is slightly more expensive than that of unscheduled property.

Many questions have occurred occur over the value of objects stolen, destroyed or lost. In anticipation of such questions, a craftmaker should maintain records of sales to establish the market price of goods and an inventory of all goods on hand. If some works are scheduled, their value must be ascertained by an expert in the field. However, this will not avoid all problems because the insurance company can always contest the scheduled value.

WHEN AND HOW TO INSURE

These are the most important issues: whether to insure or not and how to go about obtaining insurance.

DECIDING FACTORS

Three factors should be weighed to determine whether or not to obtain insurance. First, you must set a value on that which is to be insured. Life and health are of the utmost value and should always be insured. Material goods should be valued according to the cost of replacement. If you keep a large inventory of your works or if you own expensive equipment, it probably should be insured. The most elementary way to determine whether the value is sufficiently high to necessitate insurance is to rely on the pain factor: if it would hurt to lose it, insure it.

Second, you must estimate the chances that a given calamity might occur. An insurance broker can tell you what risks are most prevalent in your line of work or in your neighborhood. You should supplement this information with your own personal knowledge. For example, if your workshop is virtually fireproof and that only a massive flood would cause any real damage. These facts should be weighed in your decision, you should not be guilty of hubris for, as the great tragedians have recounted, to scoff at disaster is to invite it. If the odds are truly slim, but some risk still exists, the premium will be correspondingly smaller in most cases.

The third factor to consider is the cost of the insurance. Bear in mind that insurance purchased to cover your business is tax deductible. Theoretically, Uncle Sam is paying a percentage of the premium equal to your tax bracket.

KEEPING THE COST DOWN

As already noted, the premiums charged by an insurance company are determined by law. Nonetheless, it still pays to shop around. Insurance companies can compete by offering different packages of insurance and by hiring competent agents to assist you in your choice.

If there are enough craftmakers in your area, it may be possible for you to form a co-op insurance fund. To do this, you must estimate the total losses the co-op would sustain in the course of a year. Each member then contributes a pro rata share. The money is put into a segregated bank account to collect interest. If a major claim occurs and the losses are greater than the fund, each member must contribute pro rata to make up the difference. If at year end there is a surplus, it can be used to lessen the following year's premiums. This method is cheaper than conventional insurance because it eliminates insurance agents' commissions and whatever you would have paid toward the profit earned by the insurance company. But before you form your co-op, you should contact an attorney to determine what regulations exist in your state.

9

PRODUCT LIABILITY

In November of 1978, a California jury awarded the victim of an automobile accident $120 million after his defectively designed Ford Pinto caught fire and exploded, inflicting serious personal injury. The size of this judgment against the Ford Motor Company staggered the nation.

Unless you happen to own a Pinto, you may be thinking, "What does this have to do with me?" The answer is if you regularly sell your crafts, you might find yourself in court being sued by a customer for an injury if the customer claims that a piece you created is defective. The same laws that apply to the sale of a car by a corporation like Ford apply to a sale by an individual. In one sense it seems quite logical and fair that the laws apply equally to all regardless of size. But the law was not designed with the small business in mind.

HISTORY OF THE LIABILITY LAW

To understand the present state of liability law, it might be useful to briefly examine its roots. In 1804, a craftsman named Seixas went to a warehouse to buy some braziletto wood, supposedly a valuable wood. Mr. Woods, the warehouseman, sold

Seixas some peachum wood instead, which is virtually worthless. Neither party, apparently, knew the difference between braziletto and peachum.

When Seixas discovered the error, he tried to return the worthless wood in exchange for either braziletto or his money. The warehouseman refused because he had already given the money to the original owner of the wood. Seixas sued Woods and lost. He lost because, even though Woods had written braziletto on the invoice, he never warranted the wood as such.

The result of this case can be amply summed up by the Latin maxim *caveat emptor*: let the buyer beware. This maxim was repeated time and again in both English and American cases until comparatively recent times. But, now the pendulum has swung the other way and the rule has become *caveat vendor*: let the seller beware. The change came about gradually.

One of the harshest rules of early product liability cases was that people injured by defective products could not sue the manufacturers unless they purchased directly from them. This technical requirement was carried down the distribution lines so that only individuals who dealt with each other could have rights against each other, and consumers could not sue anyone but the retailer with whom they had traded.

This doctrine was recognized as harsh and rigid; thus, it was not followed in a number of situations. *Example*: the seller, regardless of his position in the chain of distribution, could be sued if he were negligent and the product were "inherently dangerous." The courts struggled for some time over just what was and what was not inherently dangerous.

One early case said a car was not. Supreme Court Justice Benjamin Cardozo, in a landmark decision, disagreed. To him a product was inherently dangerous if injury to the owner was predictable in cases where the item was defective. Almost anything can be injurious if defective and so the cases hold today.

Where once a car was not deemed inherently dangerous, now negligence suits have been brought for such seemingly innocuous items as a toy top, rubber boots, and a lounge chair.

Cardozo made several other important pronouncements in the field of product liability. He stated, for example, that a manufacturer could be liable for defects in component parts made by another manufacturer if the assembler did not inspect them.

This shift of the burden of responsibility from the buyer to the seller was a natural response to several factors. First, as products became increasingly more complex, it was no longer true that the buyer and seller were equally knowledgeable or ignorant. Second, it was felt that businesses were large enough to bear the immediate losses and ultimately could spread the risk over an even broader sector of society. Since the majority of the products on today's market are mass produced by large manufacturers, the present rule reflects the economic reality of industry.

This is not, however, the economic reality of the crafts market, yet it too must learn to cope with these laws in a climate of litigious consumers and generous juries. It is better to learn about these problems while you can still protect yourself than when it is too late.

PRODUCT LIABILITY

In every product liability case, the plaintiff must prove that: (1) some injury occurred to himself; (2) the injury was caused by some defect in the product; and (3) the defect was present in the product when the defendant had control over it. Once someone obtains your product, you will not be able to stop him from injuring himself, but you can control this third element by making sure that any item that leaves your control does not contain a defect.

There are two kinds of defects: mechanical defects such as loose screws, faulty component parts and so on; and design defects such as instability, flammability, toxicity, tendency to shatter and the like.

LIABILITY FOR MECHANICAL DEFECTS

The scrupulous attention to detail that is usually characteristic of handcrafted goods almost precludes the possibility of a mechanical defect. If there is a mechanical defect, it will most likely occur in a component produced by someone else.

Example: a stained glass lamp might contain a faulty electrical circuit that could cause serious injury to a user. Obviously, such a defect would be virtually impossible to detect. But, under the current rule of "strict liability," followed by most states, you can be held liable for defects that could not have been discovered or prevented by human skill, knowledge or foresight. Your only protection is insurance.

Many defects *are* detectable before an accident occurs if the right tests are made. And, as pointed out, the courts have held that manufacturers (corporate or individual) have a duty to inspect and test their goods. Failure to adequately test has been held reason enough to impose large awards of punitive damages on top of the actual damages.

TESTS AND RECORDS

How much testing is adequate? Sophisticated testing might prove to be too expensive for a craftsperson. My advice is to design the best test you can for whatever you make, even if it is only a good tug here and there and, most important, to keep a record of it. This may serve to prove that you attempted to fulfill your duty to test the product. While this precaution might not protect you from product liability, it may result in reducing, if not eliminating, punitive damage awards against you.

It is rare for an injured plaintiff to be able to prove that a defect was present when a product was purchased. The plaintiff frequently must rely on inferences drawn from the accident itself. If the jury is convinced that there is better than a fifty-fifty chance that the defect was there when the product was bought, the plaintiff will probably win. But, if you come into court with a record of tests on your product, the odds might shift in your favor.

Besides keeping records of your tests, you should also keep records of your purchases of materials and devise some method of identifying the components in your product. This way, if you are sued for a defect in a component part, you can pass the liability on to the party really at fault. For example, if a stained glass window collapses because the camming is inferior, you might be able to pass your liability on to the manufacturer of the defective cam.

DESIGN LIABILITY

The second category of defects, design defects, can be further subdivided: those that are and those that are not a violation of a statute. A 1959 case contains a good example of how far a court might go in defining a design defect. A rather obese woman entered a store and sat in a chair of contemporary design that the store had for sale. The back of the chair curved elegantly into the seat, which in turn curved down and around to form the base of the chair. It was along these serpentine curves that the overweight customer slid onto the floor. The injury to her pride was aggravated by an injury to her spine. The court held that the shape of the chair was defective and awarded her $25,000 in damages.

In defective design cases the courts have usually adhered to a common sense criterion. If the product conforms to the state of the art when it was made, it will usually not be held defective. The state of the art is *not* the same as industrywide standards. Industrywide standards may be introduced in evidence, but it cannot be assumed that these assure due care. This is because the law will not allow an industry to adopt careless practices in order to save money or time when better, more protective methods are available. State of the art, on the other hand, is the measure of how far technology in the field has advanced, and this will determine the standards for an industry.

A design may be defective if it does not meet the standards set forth in a statute. No product should be sold for consumer use before a check has been made to see whether it is covered by a consumer protection law. A violation of these laws may carry criminal sanctions. In some jurisdictions, consumers injured by a product have proven their case by merely proving that a statute was violated in the production or sale of the product. The manufacturer would then have the burden of establishing that the injury was not the result of the statutory violation, which would be almost impossible in cases where the law had been enacted to prevent the very type of injury complained of. For example, putting small lovely fastener beads on infants toys in violation of state child safety laws for such toys would expose the craft artist toymaker to liability if the infant choked on the bead.

FEDERAL LAWS

In addition to state legislation pertaining to liability, there are at least three federal laws that directly affect craftmakers. First, there is the Hazardous Substance Labeling Act as amended by the Child Protection Act of 1966 and the Child Protection and Toy Safety Act of 1969. These statutes were passed in response to the staggering number of injuries and poisonings of children under fifteen each year. Under the Hazardous Substance Labeling Act as amended, the Federal Trade Commission (FTC) is empowered to name any potentially dangerous substance a *hazardous substance*. Such substances may not be used in any product that might give a child access to the hazardous substance. That is, no amount of use or abuse by a child should make the product unsafe. Presently banned under this Act, for example, are jaquirty beans used in necklaces, jewelry and dolls' eyes. For a list of other hazardous substances, you should consult your local office of the FTC.

The second statute is the Flammable Fabrics Act. This statute empowers the FTC to establish appropriate standards of flammability for fabrics used in clothing and household products, including children's toys.

Finally, there is the Consumer Product Safety Act, a statute that empowers the FTC to regulate the composition, content and design of a consumer product. The FTC has, for example, promulgated regulations for the use of architectural glass in doors, windows and walls and has banned the use of any lead-based surface coating materials (paints). This is a dynamic area, and if there is any doubt, craftmakers should check with the FTC to determine whether the materials they use in creating craft objects are subject to regulation.

The current law of product liability has held the seller as well as the producer of a product liable. If the seller is held liable for a defective product, he may in turn seek reimbursement from the manufacturer for the amount paid in damages. This may involve another expensive suit, and, if the manufacturer is broke, the seller is out of luck. There are two things that a seller might do to protect himself. First, he can incorporate. This business method is complex and is discussed in detail in Chapter 1. The second method of self-protection is to obtain insurance.

LIABILITY INSURANCE

In general, the cost of liability insurance is affordable for the small business: $100,000 liability insurance for a person doing up to $10,000 of business a year will cost about $100 annually. Rates will vary from region to region. Craftspeople should consult their insurance brokers or agents to determine the rates in their own particular areas. Each craftsperson must then evaluate this cost against the risks of a law suit. You should know that the majority of these suits are settled for, or are litigated to, a judgment of over $100,000. You can deduct the cost of this kind of insurance as a business expense for tax purposes. Given these factors, if there is any reasonable expectation that a purchaser of your product could sustain personal injury from it, you should seriously consider obtaining product liability insurance.

The area of product liability has evolved to a point where manufacturers are being held liable for injuries caused by their defective products. The doctrines appear to have evolved with an eye to the large manufacturer of a mass produced item, but

the rules are applied with the same vigor to the craftsmaker creating a unique piece. It is, therefore, important to be aware of
the potential risks involved and to take the necessary precautions.

10

LABOR RELATIONS

There comes a time in almost every artisan's life when it is necessary to get help, be it brain or brawn. The help most commonly needed is that of a bookkeeper or accountant who can help with taxes, billing, and the like. When things get a little hectic around the shop or studio, you might hire someone to help with the packing or running errands. If selling is not your greatest talent, you may engage the services of a salesperson or a manufacturer's representative. Simply stated, the higher your sales volume, the less likely you will be able to do it yourself.

INDEPENDENT CONTRACTORS

When you hire someone on a one-time or job-by-job basis, that person is called an *independent contractor*. Although you pay for their services, such people remain their own bosses and may even subcontract others to actually do the work for you.

If you occasionally give some of your work to a friend to sell on consignment at a craft fair, the friend would be an independent contractor. If once or twice a year, you hire a bookkeeper or accountant to go over your records, that person too is an independent contractor. The fact that the person is independent, and not your employee, means that you do not have to pay Social Security taxes in addition to the cost of the work, nor do you have to withhold income taxes and observe all sorts of other rules.

More important, if, while working for you, someone is injured as a result of the independent contractor's negligence, you will generally be immune from liability. There are, however, situations where an independent contractor can render you legally responsible for his or her wrongful acts. Such situations fall into three basic categories:

• If an employer is careless in hiring an independent contractor and a careful investigation would have disclosed facts to indicate that the contractor was not qualified, the employer may be liable when the independent contractor fails to properly perform the job.

• If a job is so dangerous as to be characterized as ultra-hazardous and is to be performed for the employer's benefit, then, regardless of who performs the work, the employer will remain legally responsible for any injuries that occur during the performance of the work. Thus, a fireworks displayer, for example, cannot escape liability by having fuses lit or rockets aimed by independent contractors.

• An employer may be required by law to perform certain tasks for the health and safety of the community. These responsibilities are said to be non-delegable—that is, an employer cannot delegate them and thus escape liability for their improper performance. If, therefore, a non-delegable duty is performed by an independent contractor, the employer will remain responsible for any injury that results. A good example of a non-delegable duty is the law (common in many states) that homeowners are responsible for keeping their sidewalks free of dangerous obstacles. If a homeowner hires an independent contractor to fulfill this obligation by removing ice during the winter, the homeowner may still be legally liable to someone injured on the slippery sidewalk, even if the accident resulted from the contractor's carelessness.

EMPLOYEES

The second capacity in which someone can work for you is that of *employee*. This category includes anyone over whose work you exercise direct control—helpers, apprentices, salespeople who represent you alone, a bookkeeper who is a full-time or regular part-time member of your staff are examples.

The formation of this relationship entails nothing more than an agreement on your side to hire someone and an agreement by that person to work for you. Although a written contract is not necessary except in the case of employment for more than one year, putting down employment terms in writing, so that there is no misunderstanding later is always a good idea.

EMPLOYMENT CONTRACTS

If the employment is to be for more than one year, then there must be a written contract specifying the period of employment; otherwise, either party may terminate the relationship at any time. While there is no prescribed form that the contract must take, there are certain items that should be considered. The first item of an employment contract is the term of employment. An employment contract may be either terminable at will or for a fixed duration. Making the contract for a fixed period gives the employee some job security and creates a moral and contractual obligation for the employee to remain for the term. Of course, if the employee chooses to quit, or the employer chooses to fire the employee, the law will not compel fulfillment of the contract. That went out with selling orphans into apprenticeships and other forms of slavery.

The second item is the wage. Unless you are a large employer with forty-five or more employees, or are engaged in interstate commerce (which is defined as having gross sales of $500,000 or more), you will not have to comply with federal minimum-wage laws, but most states have their own minimum wages, which must be paid. Other than the requirement imposed by this law, the amount of remuneration is open to bargaining.

In addition to an hourly wage or monthly salary, other benefits can be given, such as health and life insurance or retirement pensions. Some legal advice may be necessary here in order to take advantage of tax laws. In the event no salary is specified, the law will presume a reasonable wage for the work performed. Thus, you cannot escape paying your employees by not discussing the amount they will earn. If you hire a glassblower and the accepted salary in your region for a person qualified to blow glass is $10 per hour, then it is presumed that the glassblower is hired for this amount unless you and that person have agreed to a different salary.

Third, it is often wise to spell out your employee's duties in the employment contract. This serves as a form of orientation for the employee and also may limit future conflicts over what is and what is not involved in the job.

Fourth, you may want your employee to agree not to work for someone else while working for you or, more important, not to compete against you at the end of the employment period. The latter agreement must be carefully drawn to be enforceable. Such an agreement must not be overly broad in the kind of work the employee may not do; it must cover a geographic area no broader than that in which you actually operate; and it must be for a reasonable duration—a five-year period has been upheld.

Finally, grounds for termination of the employment contract should be listed. Even if the contract is terminable at will, these grounds serve as useful benchmarks to guide your employee's actions.

Unlike the independent contractor, you are liable for the negligence and, sometimes, even the intentional wrongdoing of your employee when the employee is acting on your behalf. This means that if your employee is on the job and is involved in an automobile accident that is his or her fault, you may be held responsible. It would be wise to be extremely careful when hiring, and to contact your insurance agent to obtain sufficient insurance coverage for your additional exposure.

OTHER CONSIDERATIONS IN HIRING

There are other issues you should consider when hiring an employee, most of which fall into the realm of accounting or bookkeeping responsibilities. You should, therefore, consult with your accountant or bookkeeper regarding such items as:

1. A worker's compensation policy for your employees in the event of on-the-job injury. State laws vary on the minimum number of employees an employer must have before obtaining such a policy.
2. Withholding taxes: federal, state and local. Here, too, the laws vary, and you are urged to find out what is required in your locale.
3. Social Security (FICA). There are some exemptions from this body of social legislation. Contact your local Social Security office to determine how these exemptions may affect you.
4. Unemployment insurance, both federal and state. These also include certain technical requirements for subcontractors and the like.
5. Health and safety regulations, both federal and state.
6. Municipal taxes for specific programs such as schools or public transportation.
7. Miscellaneous employee benefits such as insurance coverage (medical, dental, legal), parking, retirement benefits, memberships, etc.
8. Union requirements, if you or your employees are subject to union contracts.
9. Wage and hour laws, both federal and state. These include minimum wage and overtime requirements. In some states the law regulates holiday and vacation requirements, as well as the method of paying employees during employment and upon termination.

As already noted, the requirements of these laws may vary

dramatically from state to state, and craftspeople are well advised to discuss them with their accountants or bookkeepers. In addition, you should find out whether any other forms of employment legislation, such as licensing requirements, apply to you, your employees, or your business by consulting an attorney experienced in your type of business. You could also contact the clerk in your municipality.

11

ON GETTING PAID FOR YOUR WORK

It is axiomatic that craftspeople who sell their work must wear two hats—as craftspeople and as business people. This may be distasteful to some, but it is, nevertheless, necessary if you want to realize the fruit of your labors.

COLLECTION PROBLEMS

It is difficult enough to make a sale—either directly to the ultimate client or consumer, or through a retail store or gallery. In either case, collection problems can and do occur. There are several methods to deal with these problems, ranging from preventive action to initiating a lawsuit.

The general rule in a sales transaction is that payment is due upon delivery of the item being sold. While this rule may be subject to some technical complications beyond the scope of this discussion, it means that when work is delivered to a customer, the seller has the legal right to demand payment in full at that moment. This assumes that no arrangement has been made between the buyer and the seller that would allow the purchaser to delay payment.

While payment upon delivery is common in retail transactions, it is unusual when selling through a dealer or gallery. In addition, the purchase of a rather expensive item may be subject to an installment sale arrangement.

If you are fortunate enough to deal with people who always pay their bills on time, then the remaining portion of this chapter may be of no concern to you. However, if you have experienced delays in payment, or have had some totally uncollectible bills, then the suggestions that follow should prove useful.

PAYMENT: AFTER WORK IS SOLD, OR AFTER AN INVOICE IS SUBMITTED

If you sell through a dealer, there are at least two possible arrangements. First, the craftwork may be consigned and payment is due only after the work is actually sold. Unfortunately, it is not uncommon for a dealer to neglect informing a craftsperson of a sale, or to delay notification for an unreasonably long period of time. In recent years, many retail outlets were forced into bankruptcy, thus subjecting the craftsperson to the possible loss of works. (For more detailed information, refer to Chapter 4, which deals with the legal ramifications of consignment selling, with suggestions for protective steps that can be taken under the Uniform Commercial Code, especially in states where specific consignment protection legislation does not exist.)

The other method of doing business is for the craftsperson to be paid after submitting an invoice to the wholesale buyer. Commonly, invoices are payable within a specified time, usually thirty days after they have been tendered. Unfortunately, this system virtually guarantees that the craftsperson will not receive payment until the invoice is due. Indeed, unless some inducement for early payment is offered, the craftsperson may wait interminably to be paid.

WAYS OF ENCOURAGING PAYMENT

CASH DISCOUNTS

A simple way to encourage early payment is to offer cash discounts. The offer of a five percent cash discount for early or even on-time payment may be all the encouragement some purchasers need. If the dealer is earning more interest on his cash reserves than is offered as a discount, however, the cash discount has no appeal.

CHARGING INTEREST ON OVERDUE PAYMENTS: PROS AND CONS

The other option, which can be combined with the incentive of cash discounts, is to charge interest on payment past the invoice due date. This method contains two possible traps. First, many states still have usury laws that limit the percent of interest that can be charged. A lender who exceeds the legal interest ceiling may find that the entire debt is forfeited, or all interest is forfeited, or that a usury penalty is imposed.

The second possible problem is the necessity to comply with the federal Truth-in-Lending Act and the various equivalent state laws. On the face of it, a law called Truth-in-Lending would not seem to be applicable to a craftsperson selling works, but the law applies to every transaction in which interest or a finance charge is imposed. The Truth-in-Lending Act is basically a disclosure law, requiring that certain terms be included on any contract or billing that charges interest. The disclosures have been simplified recently and the task of compliance is further eased by the availability of pre-printed forms that contain the required disclosures. While many of the required terms may seem to be inapplicable to a simple sales transaction, if you want to charge interest, then you would be well advised to use a form that contains all the disclosures. These forms are available from legal publishers, the Volunteer Lawyers for the Arts organizations in the various states, or a private attorney.

IF THE PAYMENT NEVER COMES...

If neither the carrot nor the stick is effective in obtaining payment, you have several methods by which to proceed. The first possibility is to do nothing. If the amount is small enough, you may simply decide not to pursue collection. Needless to say, if this alternative is selected, you should refrain from doing any future business with that customer.

LAWSUIT

A second option is the instigation of a full-scale lawsuit to force payment. Under the rules in many states, a formal demand for payment must be made prior to commencing a lawsuit. This option is only practical if the outstanding debt is relatively large. An attorney must be hired and will likely be quite expensive, particularly if the case goes to trial.

Also, the fees charged for filing a case are rather high and the debtor must be personally served with notice of the suit. This is most often done by hiring a process server, another expensive proposition. Lastly, if the case is won and the buyer still refuses to pay, further proceedings must be initiated to force payment. All in all, the expense involved in a civil trial may amount to more than the debt itself.

SMALL CLAIMS COURT

A simpler and less expensive option is to bring an action in small claims court. While the rules vary from state to state, all of the systems are geared toward making the process as swift, accessible and inexpensive as possible. Moreover, most courts have staff members who help guide people through pleading and practice in small claims court.

The major savings in a small claims court proceeding is the fact that attorneys are not customarily permitted in such courts. Unless they represent themselves or a corporation, attorneys are not allowed generally to assist with completion of the necessary forms, nor to appear in court. Even in states where attorneys are not specifically barred by statute, the court rules are set up in such a clear, comprehensible way that an attorney is usually not needed.

A small claims suit has other advantages over a conventional lawsuit. Not all actions, however, can be brought in small claims court. As the name implies, only claims for small amounts can be brought. The definition of *small* ranges from up to $500 in Arizona to up to $2,500 in Illinois. Moreover, only suits for monetary damages are appropriate for small claims court; other forms of relief, such as an injunction or specific performance, cannot be granted.

Once initiated, the small claims court process is relatively swift and inexpensive. Filing fees are generally under $35. In some states, such as Arizona, if the claim is extremely small (under $50), there is no filing fee at all. In addition, in most courts, the creditor is not responsible for informing the debtor that suit has been brought. The clerk of the court customarily mails the notice to the defendant by certified or registered mail. A small fee is generally charged to cover mailing costs.

In many states, the hearing on a small claims action may be held on weekends or evenings. The procedure in the hearing itself is meant to be quite simple. The technical rules of evidence and of legal procedure are not followed. The judge simply hears both sides of the case and allows the testimony of any witnesses or evidence either party has to offer. Jury trials are never permitted in small claims court, although the defendant may be able to have the case moved to a conventional court if he desires a trial by jury.

An action in small claims court has certain disadvantages. First, the judgment is often absolutely binding: neither party may appeal. Where appeal is allowed, as in New York State, the party wishing to challenge the judgment must show that a grave injustice has been done. This is not easy.

The other major disadvantage of a small claims action is that the judgment may be uncollectible. In many states the usual methods of enforcing a judgment—garnishment of wages or liens against property—are unavailable to the holder of a judgment from small claims court. In other states, New York, for example, enforcement action can only be taken if the debt involved is the result of a business transaction and the debtor has three other outstanding small claims court judgments.

For the most part, careful screening of customers will minimize the need to use legal means to collect payment for sales. However, if all other methods fail, small claims court is by far the least expensive and easiest way to obtain legal redress for an outstanding debt. It does, nevertheless, have some drawbacks that should be considered before you decide to use it as a remedy.

POINT·OF·SALE PAYMENTS

Craftspeople who deal directly with the public at craft shows, fairs, or at their own shops customarily expect to be paid at the moment they make the sale, before the craftwork is taken away by the customer. Such payment is made by currency, check, or credit card. It is, therefore, necessary for the craftsperson to determine whether the currency is authentic, whether the check is going to be paid by the bank, or whether the credit card will be honored.

CURRENCY

Identifying counterfeit currency is usually very technical and difficult. Occasionally, however, it is simple if the counterfeiter has made a glaring error, such as using George Washington on a five-dollar bill. Much more subtle irregularities are more likely the norm. The federal government is quite diligent in alerting businesspeople to the presence of counterfeit currency in a particular area when it is aware of the problem. The best way to avoid being stuck with a counterfeit bill is to keep your eyes open. Also, do not accept very large bills, for example $100 or more.

CREDIT CARDS

To avoid credit card fraud, the first thing to do is to compare the signature on the back of the card with the signature on the transaction slip. Even more important is to follow the credit card company's procedures carefully. If the company requires you to get authorization for all credit card sales over $50, then be sure to get that authorization. This may seem time-consuming and troublesome, but the rules are well grounded. If you have made a credit card sale without following the instructions, and the credit card turns out to have been stolen or otherwise invalid, or the buyer has exceeded his or her credit limit, you are likely to be stuck with the loss.

PERSONAL CHECKS

The most frequent difficulty occurs when personal checks are used in payment. A host of things can prevent a check from being honored or cashed by a bank. To begin with, the person who writes the check may be an imposter, using a checkbook that actually belongs to someone else. In order to reduce the likelihood of this occurrence, craftspeople should insist upon seeing at least two pieces of identification, one of which should, ideally, contain a photograph of the person. Many states require drivers to have photographs on their drivers' licenses. A current major credit card, or a check guarantee card with photo and signature facsimile are also good. Do not accept as identification such items as a Social Security card, a library card, or any ID that can be easily obtained or forged.

Again, watch while the person signs the check (signatures may have been previously traced from a valid signature), and compare the signature with the signature on the other identification. While only an expert can identify a good forgery, clumsy attempts by amateurs may be easily recognized.

To further protect yourself, accept checks only if they are made out to you and only if they are written for the exact amount of the sale. In other words, do not take checks made out to someone else and endorsed to you, never *cash* a check, and do not take checks for more than the sale amount.

Even if the individual writing the check is legitimate, other possible problems still exist. One of the most common difficulties is the problem of insufficient funds to cover the check. If the amount of your sale is substantial, it would be prudent to request a certified or bank guaranteed check. This, however, may deter impulse purchases, and is thus not practical for most craftspeople and craft retailers.

If the person writing the check is known to the recipient, the risk of having a check bounce is minimal. If, however, the craft sale is to a stranger, the risk of receiving a bad check can be reduced if the purchaser's address and phone number are copied onto the check from the supporting pieces of identification, even if they are also printed on the check. One should also be wary of an individual presenting a check from a bank well beyond the local area, vacationers not withstanding.

Despite all these precautions, some bad checks do slip through. In most states it is a crime to obtain property by using a bad check. In addition, if the person can be found, a lawsuit can be brought to recover the amount of the check. If you win the suit, most states will allow the recovery of reasonable costs of litigation, including reasonable attorney's fees.

PROBLEMS WITH PAYMENTS FROM GALLERIES

Most craftspeople do not operate their own retail shops; rather, they market their work through other outlets, such as stores and galleries. With gallery owners, it is common practice to take a work on consignment and to pay for it after it has ultimately been sold. As discussed in Chapter 4, craftspeople should always use contracts when consigning work, specifying what has been consigned, what the financial arrangement is, when the work is to be paid for, how long it is to remain on consignment, who is responsible for insurance, and so forth. Many states now have laws regulating the relationship between creative people and the galleries with which they deal.

GALLERY BANKRUPTCY

Some of these laws were enacted as a result of an unfortunate scenario that has occurred with alarming regularity during the past several years. Artists and craftspeople would consign their work to a gallery, expecting to be paid within a reasonable time or to have their work returned in good condition, and would learn sometime later that the gallery had gone bankrupt.

When a bankruptcy petition is filed, the court appoints a trustee who is responsible for assembling all the assets of the bankrupt and notifying all creditors of the proceeding. The trustee represents the bankrupt until the proceeding is concluded.

Craftspeople who have work on consignment in a gallery are among the creditors if that gallery goes bankrupt. But, many craftspeople do nothing when they receive the required notification from the bankruptcy court, and thus they get nothing. It is far wiser to reply to the request for information from the bankruptcy trustee and to appear at any creditors' meetings. Craftspeople could get together and appoint one of their number as the deputy for purposes of appearing at creditors' meetings, or they could pool their resources and hire an attorney for this purpose, especially if the meeting is in another city or state. This will, of course, cost some money. If the amount at stake in the bankruptcy is small, it may not be economically practical to pursue the matter.

PRECAUTIONS: CONSIGNMENT LAWS

The most prudent way to deal with the possibility of a gallery becoming insolvent is to take some precautions before the event occurs. Many states have special laws dealing with consignments, and those laws set up some form of protection for creative people who consign their works. Article 9 of the Uniform Commercial Code, which has been adopted in every state of the United States, also contains a procedure whereby craftspeople can fill out a form called a UCC-1, file it with the appropriate government office (set forth in the form), and obtain secured protection in the consigned work while it is in the gallery.

It should be noted that every state form is slightly different and therefore it is essential to use the form bearing the name of the state in which you are filing. The document must be filed in the state where the consigned work is to be located. The purpose of this filing is to establish a public record and inform all gallery creditors that the works that appear in its inventory are, in fact, owned by others. Remember, when you consign work, the work is still your property, even though it is on the gallery's premises waiting to be sold.

If you have filed the proper, signed UCC documents to establish your security interest covering the *full* value of the work, and then the gallery to which you have consigned the work goes bankrupt, all your work will be returned to you. However, if for some reason the security interest you have established is for less than the full value of the work, the bankruptcy trustee may sell the items and pay you only the amount of the security interest that your UCC documents indicate.

BANKRUPTCIES

STRAIGHT BANKRUPTCY

There are two general categories of bankruptcy. The first, referred to as *straight bankruptcy* in Chapter 7 of the Bankruptcy Law, contemplates the prompt conversion of all of the bankrupt's nonexempt property to cash, and the payment of creditors. The Bankruptcy Law establishes a hierarchy of creditors, giving some creditors priority for payment. Such creditors would be the U.S. government for taxes, and secured parties for the amount of their security interests. Each category of creditor must be paid in full before a lower priority creditor may be paid at all. If there is not sufficient money to satisfy all creditors in a particular class, the members of that group will receive a *pro rata* portion of their claim.

As noted above, not all of the bankrupt's assets are available for creditors. There are some things that may be retained, such as a modest house, a holy book, clothing, and the like, even after bankruptcy. The list of exempt property varies from state to state.

After the bankrupt's nonexempt assets are completely distributed, the trustee will apply to the bankruptcy judge for a discharge order. If the bankrupt has fulfilled all requirements of the Bankruptcy Law, and the judge is satisfied with the proceeding, the bankrupt's debts then will be wiped out—or *discharged*—and the proceeding will end. Certain claims cannot be discharged in bankruptcy. For example, a creditor who was not notified of the meeting and given a chance to participate will have a claim that remains viable even after the bankruptcy proceeding has ended.

REORGANIZATION

The second type of bankruptcy proceeding is the so-called *Chapter 11*, or *reorganization*, contemplating a somewhat different process. Rather than terminating the business, a Chapter 11 is designed to facilitate an orderly payment to creditors so that the business may survive.

When the Chapter 11 petition is filed and the creditors meet, a reorganization plan is proposed. All legal proceedings for debt collection other than the bankruptcy proceeding are frozen, and the bankrupt is given an opportunity to satisfy the creditors in a timely fashion. Once a plan acceptable to all creditors is prepared, it is presented to the bankruptcy judge. If it is determined that the Chapter 11 reorganization plan is "fair and equitable," the judge will approve it and it will be implemented.

Creditors customarily receive more under Chapter 11 than they do under straight bankruptcy, although reorganization is feasible only when a healthy business is suffering from a temporary economic reversal. Creditors who have a secured position, such as those who have filed UCC documents to establish their security interest (discussed above), do participate in drafting the Chapter 11 plan. If the plan meets any of the three following tests, it will be "fair and equitable" so far as the secured creditors are concerned, and they may be forced to agree:

- The secured creditors retain their liens and receive future cash payments equal to the value of the security;
- The secured parties retain a lien on the proceeds from the sale of their collateral; or
- They receive the equivalent of their interests, such as cash up front or substituted collateral.

In a Chapter 11 proceeding, a secured creditor may be forced to take a less favorable position than the Uniform Commercial Code would allow in order to have the plan accepted by all the creditors. Even though that may happen on occasion, a craftsperson with a security interest is still far better off than one who is unsecured.

Common sense, diligence, and attention to detail are always important attributes for any businessperson. When the economy is weak and money is tight, they become essential. There will probably always be some deadbeats and some uncollectible bills. But with proper care and some preventative maintenance, you can keep these to a minimum.

12

HOW TO FIND A LAWYER

"I want to see a lawyer!"

That plaintive cry is heard most often when someone gets into a peck of trouble. But most lawyers are not Perry Masons, keeping people out of jail by dint of clairvoyant detective work and a facile courtroom oration. And most people, fortunately, do not need lawyers for so serious a purpose.

However, it is a rare individual who gets through an entire lifetime without ever needing a lawyer, particularly businesspeople. A lawyer, like a doctor, is as essential in *preventing* problems before they arise, as in solving them afterwards.

Like doctors or craftspeople, lawyers specialize. Because the law has become so diverse and intricate, some lawyers handle only corporation law, others specialize in divorce, still others take only criminal cases, and so forth. Yet, there are still thousands of "general practitioners" who are well-versed in the normal, ordinary problems most of us face: buying or selling a house, making a will, signing a contract, setting up a business venture. Of course, you do not need legal advice every time you sign something. A contract for a booth at a craft fair, for example, is hardly worth the expense of a legal consultation.

WHEN TO GET A LAWYER

The New York State Bar Association provides this rule of thumb: "Get a lawyer's advice whenever you run into serious problems concerning your freedom, your financial situation, your domestic affairs, or your property." The word *serious* is the important one in that sentence.

Legal matters fall into two basic classifications: civil cases and criminal cases.

Civil cases concern disputes between two parties, such as breach of contract, non-performance of an obligation, and the like. A lawyer is necessary in such cases to protect your rights. In your business and personal affairs a lawyer helps to prevent complications that could end up in court as civil cases.

Criminal cases concern violations of the criminal law, such as murder, theft, forgery and the like. In such cases the government accuses a person of committing a specific crime.

Under our legal system, it is presumed that a person is innocent until proven guilty. It provides that every criminal defendant is entitled to a lawyer, even if the government has to pay the lawyer's fees because the defendant does not have the resources to hire a lawyer.

If you are ever confronted with a criminal matter that could lead to loss of liberty or property, the first call you should make is to a lawyer. Do not ever plead guilty to anything (except, perhaps, a parking ticket) without consulting a lawyer first. What may seem insignificant to you could well lead to serious consequences if you do not have proper legal advice.

DISCUSS FEES

When discussing a case with a lawyer, do not hesitate to discuss the fee as well. Fees generally depend upon the amount of time and research involved in the case. With simple matters, such as incorporating a business or drawing up a will, a fee can easily be determined since your lawyer will know approximately how much time will be necessary. More complicated cases may require an estimate, which will give you a general idea of the possible cost.

Some cases, especially law suits involving the recovery of money in accident cases, are often handled on a *contingency-fee* basis. This means the lawyer gets 25 to 50 percent of the amount if the case is won, but gets nothing if the case is lost. Even in lost case, however, the court costs have to be paid by the client.

The relations between a lawyer and a client are by law held to be confidential. A lawyer cannot be compelled—and indeed, is not permitted—to reveal what has been discussed with a client without the client's permission. But you should realize that this confidential relationship exists to enable the lawyer to get all the information necessary, even such information as may be unfavorable to the client. It is the only way the lawyer can properly prepare a case and can properly represent the client.

WHERE TO FIND A LAWYER

Where do you find a good lawyer?

Since all lawyers are licensed, it is a matter of finding someone in whom you can have confidence, much as you would find a doctor or any other professional you trust. Ask friends or business acquaintances to recommend someone they have found to be satisfactory. You may want to talk to several lawyers before you settle on someone with whom you can establish that special relationship of confidence. The local bar association may be able to recommend someone if you have a problem that requires specialized legal experience.

If your resources are very limited, the Legal Aid Society (or its local equivalent in your area) may be of help. For information and possibly free legal service on problems related specifically to your work as a crafts producer, contact Volunteer Lawyers for the Arts, which has chapters in many states. If you cannot find them in your phone book or through your local bar association, write to Volunteer Lawyers for the Arts, 1560 Broadway, Suite 711, New York, NY 10036. Their phone number is (212) 575-1150.

The better part of wisdom is to have a lawyer before you need one. And sooner or later, you will probably need one.

VOLUNTEER LAWYERS FOR THE ARTS

Volunteer Lawyers for the Arts—VLA—was founded in New York City in 1969 to provide artists and arts organizations with the legal assistance they needed but were not able to afford. Subsequently, other VLA-type organizations were established throughout the United States. Each VLA chapter is different. Some offer seminars, conferences, and newsletters; others provide accounting and business advice; some have financial requirements for eligibility; and some charge minimal fees for services. For a comprehensive list, see page 139.

VOLUNTEER LAWYER ORGANIZATIONS

ALABAMA
Alabama Lawyers for the Arts
   (ALA)
267 Childester Ave.
Mobile, Alabama 36607
(205) 471-2434

CALIFORNIA
California Lawyers for the Arts
   (CLA)
Fort Mason Center
Building C, Rm 255
San Francisco, California 94123
(415) 755-1143

Los Angeles office:
315 West 9th Street, # 1101
Los Angeles, California 90015
(213) 623-8311

San Diego Lawyers for the Arts
1205 Prospect Street, # 400
La Jolla, California 92037
(619) 454-9696

COLORADO
Colorado Lawyers for the Arts
   (COLA)
P.O. Box 300428
Denver, Colorado 80203
(303) 892-7122

CONNECTICUT
Connecticut Commission on the
   Arts (CTVLA)
227 Lawrence Street
Hartford, Connecticut 06106
(203) 566-4770

DISTRICT OF COLUMBIA
District of Columbia Lawyers
   Committee for the Arts,
   Volunteer Lawyers for the
   Arts, D.C.
918 Sixteenth Street, N.W., # 503
Washington, D.C. 20006
(202) 429-0229

Washington Area Lawyers for the
Arts (WALA)
1325 G Street, NW - Lower Level
Washington, D.C. 20006
(202) 393-2826

FLORIDA
Volunteer Lawyers for the
Arts/Broward and Business
Volunteer Lawyers for the
Arts/Broward, Inc.
5900 Nth Andrews Avenue, # 907
Fort Lauderdale, Florida 33309
(305) 771-4131

Business Volunteers for the
Arts/Miami (BVA)
150 West Flagler Street, # 2500
Miami, Florida 33130
(305) 789-3590

GEORGIA
Georgia Volunteer Lawyers for the
Arts (GVLA)
2330 34 Peachtree Street, NW
Atlanta, Georgia 30303
(404) 525-6046

ILLINOIS
Lawyers for the Creative Arts
(LCA)
213 West Institute Place, # 411
Chicago, Illinois 60610
(312) 944-ARTS

KANSAS
Kansas Register of Volunteers for
the Arts (KRVA)
c/o Susan J. Whitfield-Lungren,
Esq.
400 N. Woodlawn
East Building, # 212
Wichita, Kansas 67028
(316) 686-1155

KENTUCKY
Arts Council Services
623 West Main Street
Louisville, Kentucky 40202
(502) 582-0149

Lexington Arts & Cultural Council
Dee Peretz, Executive Director
ArtsPlace
161 North Mill Street
Lexington, Kentucky 40507
(606) 255-2951

LOUISIANA
Louisiana Volunteer Lawyers for
the Arts (LVLA)
c/o Arts Council of New Orleans
821 Gravier Street, # 600
New Orleans, Louisiana 70112
(504) 523-1465

MAINE
Maine Arts Commission
55 Capitol Street
State House Station 25
Augusta, Maine 04333
(207) 289-2724

MARYLAND
Maryland Lawyers for the Arts
Belvedere Hotel
1 East Chase Street, # 1118
Baltimore, Maryland 21202-2526
(301) 752-1633

MASSACHUSETTS
The Arts Extension Service (AES)
Division of Continuing Education
University of Massachusetts
Amherst, Massachusetts 01003
(413) 545-2360

Lawyers for the Arts
The Artists Foundation, Inc.
8 Park Plaza
Boston, Massachusetts 02116
(617) 227-2787

MINNESOTA
Resources and Counseling, United
Arts
429 Landmark Center
75 West 5th Street
St. Paul, Minnesota 55102
(612) 292-3206

MISSOURI
St. Louis Volunteer Lawyers and
Accountants
for the Arts (SLVLAA)
3540 Washington
St. Louis, Missouri 63103
(314) 652-2410

Kansas City Attorneys for the Arts
Rosalee M. MCNamara
Gage & Tucker
2345 Grand Avenue
Kansas City, Missouri 64141
(816) 474-6460

MONTANA
Montana Volunteer Lawyers for the
Arts
c/o Jean Jonkel,Esq.
P.O. Box 8687
Missoula, Montana 59807
(406) 721-1835

NEW JERSEY
Volunteer Lawyers for the Arts of
New Jersey. A special project
Center for Non-Profit
Corporations
36 West Lafayette Street
Trenton, New Jersey 08608
(609) 695-6422

NEW YORK
Volunteer Lawyers for the Arts
Program
Albany League of Arts (ALA)
19 Clinton Avenue
Albany, New York 12207

Huntington Arts Council, Inc.
213 Main Street
Huntington, New York 11743
(516) 271-8423

Volunteer Lawyers for the Arts
(VLA)
1285 Avenue of the Americas,
Third Floor
New York, New York 10019
(212) 245-4514

Arts Council in Buffalo and Erie
County
Karen Kosman, Program
Coordinator
700 Main Street
Buffalo, New York 64141
(716) 856-7520

NORTH CAROLINA
North Carolina Volunteer Lawyers
for the Arts
P.O. Box 26484
Raleigh, North Carolina 27611-
6484
(919) 741-7508

OHIO
Volunteer Lawyers and
Accountants for the Arts
(VLAA), c/o The Cleveland
Bar Association
113 St. Clair Avenue
Cleveland, Ohio 44114-1253
(216) 696-3525

Toledo Volunteer Lawyers for the
Arts
421-A N. Michigan Street
Toledo, Ohio 43624
(419) 243-3125

OKLAHOMA
Oklahoma Accountants and
Lawyers for the Arts
3000 Pershing Blvd
Oklahoma, Oklahoma 73107
(405) 948-6401

PENNSYLVANIA
Philadelphia Volunteer Lawyers
for the Arts (PVLA)
251 South 18th Street
Philadelphia, Pennsylvania 19103
(215) 545-3385

RHODE ISLAND
Ocean State Lawyers for the Arts
(OSLA)
P.O. Box 19
Saunderstown, Rhode Island
02874
(401) 789-5686

TENNESSEE
Tennessee Arts Commission
Bennett Tarleton
320 Sixth Avenue N.
Nashville, Tennessee 37219
(615) 741-1701

TEXAS
Austin Lawyers and Accountants
and Lawyers for the Arts
(ALAA)
P.O. Box 2577
Austin, Texas 78768
(512) 476-7573

Texas Accountants and Lawyers for
the Arts/Dallas
5151 Belt Line Road, #1005
Dallas, Texas 75240
(214) 701-8275

Texas Accountants and Lawyers for
the Arts (TALA)
1540 Sul Ross
Huston, Texas 77006
(713) 526-4876

UTAH

Utah Lawyers for the Arts (ULA)
170 South Main Street, # 1400
Salt Lake City, Utah 84101
(801) 521-3200

WASHINGTON

Washington Lawyers for the Arts
(WLA)
1331 Third Avenue, #512
Seattle, Washington 98101
(206) 223-0502

OTHER VOLUNTEER LAWYERS GROUPS

CANADA

Canadian Artists' Representation
Ontario (CARO)
183 Bathurst St., 1st Floor
Toronto, Ontario M5T 2R7
Canada
(416) 360-0780

PUERTO RICO

Voluntarios Por Las
Artes/Volunteers for the Arts
563 Trigo Street
El Dorado Blvd., # 5-B
Miramar, Puerto Rico 00907
(809) 721-7720

INDEX